Entered according to Act of the Parliament of Canada, in the year one thousand
nine hundred and five, by THE COPP, CLARK COMPANY, LIMITED, Toronto,
Ontario, in the Office of the Minister of Agriculture.

INTRODUCTION.

IN the ten years that have elapsed since the High School Chemistry was issued there have been important changes both in the curriculum and in the character of educational work which have made a revision of the book necessary. Some preliminary scientific training will fit students to take up the Chemistry of the Middle School at a stage considerably in advance of that which formerly was possible. The view has become prevalent, too, that Chemistry, apart altogether from the knowledge of facts and theories which it requires, may be made a subject of high educational value if properly used.

In preparing this revised text book, attention has been given to this aspect of chemical teaching by attempting to guide the pupil as to what are the essential features to be observed in the various processes, and what conclusions may legitimately be drawn from them; also, by frequent references to the relationships of methods and materials to industrial operations that the students are likely to be acquainted with, or interested in.

It must not be forgotten, however, that a book of this kind is intended to be only an agency which the teacher may use to make his work more effective; and the school programme anticipates teaching in chemistry, not the mere learning of facts.

KINGSTON, May 1st, 1905.

CONTENTS

CHAPTER I
Historical—Before Chemistry. 1

CHAPTER II
Physical and Chemical Changes 4

CHAPTER III.
Conditions that Promote Chemical Change 11

CHAPTER IV
Theory of Chemical Action 17

CHAPTER V.
Elements 21

CHAPTER VI
To Find out if Water is an Element 24

CHAPTER VII.
The Preparation and Properties of Hydrogen . . 26

CHAPTER VIII.
Chemical Notation 37

CHAPTER IX
Oxygen 42

CHAPTER X.
Oxidation and Reduction 49

CONTENTS.

CHAPTER XI.
Hydrogen Dioxide or Peroxide 52

CHAPTER XII
Ozone 54

CHAPTER XIII
Nascent State 56

CHAPTER XIV.
Acids, Bases and Salts 58

CHAPTER XV
Chemical Nomenclature 62

CHAPTER XVI
Valency 64

CHAPTER XVII
Synthesis of Water 70

CHAPTER XVIII.
Definite Proportions 76

CHAPTER XIX
Some Chemical Calculations 79

CHAPTER XX
Combustion 81

CHAPTER XXI
Is Air an Element, a Compound or a Mixture of Gases? 84

CHAPTER XXII
Nitrogen: Its Properties and Preparation 90

CONTENTS.

CHAPTER XXIII
Compounds of Nitrogen and Oxygen 92

CHAPTER XXIV
Acids of Nitrogen 101

CHAPTER XXV.
Nitrogen and Hydrogen 107

CHAPTER XXVI
Percentage Composition and Formulas 116

CHAPTER XXVII
Carbon 123

CHAPTER XXVIII.
Carbon Compounds 128

CHAPTER XXIX
Density of Gases 144

CHAPTER XXX
Carbon and Hydrogen 148

CHAPTER XXXI.
Coal Gas and Flame 152

CHAPTER XXXII
Chlorine 160

CHAPTER XXXIII
Hydrochloric Acid 165

CHAPTER XXXIV
Bleaching Powder 170

CONTENTS.

CHAPTER XXXV.

	PAGE
Sulphur	176

CHAPTER XXXVI

| Oxides of Sulphur | 179 |

CHAPTER XXXVII.

| Hydrogen and Sulphur | 181 |

CHAPTER XXXVIII

| Acids of Sulphur | 183 |

CHAPTER XXXIX

| Calculation of Formulas | 188 |

CHAPTER XL.

| Impurities in Air and Water | 189 |

CHAPTER XLI

| Molecules of Elements Usually Consist of More than One Atom | 192 |

CHAPTER XLII

| Theory of Dissociation in Solution | 197 |

CHAPTER XLIII

| Historical—The Beginnings of Chemistry | 203 |
| Appendix | 205 |

HIGH SCHOOL CHEMISTRY.

CHAPTER I

Historical—Before Chemistry.

ALCHEMY.

Chemistry, as a science, is just one hundred years old, for it was in 1802-4 that Dalton, the Manchester physician, was working out his famous Atomic Theory, which affords a basis for an orderly and systematic arrangement of the matter and the methods that have grown into chemical science. It does not follow, however, that facts and methods, as we know them, have all come into existence, or into the knowledge of men, within the last hundred years. Twenty-three centuries before Dalton, Greek philosophers had formulated a theory of the constitution of matter not very different from the modern one; and a great body of speculations and of facts came drifting down through the ages, growing in volume, and tending more toward experimental exactness as it became older It was passed on from generation to generation by men, keen of brain, earnest of purpose, ambitious for discovery, working, dreaming, hoping some day to gain the coveted knowledge of the agency that could change all inanimate things into a more perfect state.

Greek and Roman philosophers held and taught various theories regarding matter; but, with the revival of learning, these had generally taken the form that different kinds of matter, as the metals, rocks, soils, air, etc, existed because each had an essence or principle of its own; and, with suitable treatment, those kinds that were less perfect might be improved; for example, that all metals might be changed to gold if the proper agency were applied. The men who were engaged in the effort to transmute the baser sorts of matter into more perfect ones were the **alchemists**, and their system was **alchemy,** the predecessor of modern chemistry.

Gunpowder, printing, dyeing, glass staining, and many operations in metals had their origin during the time when there was no chemistry, and many of the useful applications of material things to the processes of life sprang directly from the work of alchemists. Roger Bacon, Basil Valentine, Geber, Albertus Magnus, and Paracelsus are some of the noted names connected with the systems of alchemy.

PHLOGISTON.

Some men during the 17th century became dissatisfied with the theory of essences and transmutations as a means of explaining the large number of experimental results that had accumulated   Boyle, in England (1624-1691), Rey, in France, and Stahl, in Germany (1660-1724), were leaders in the attempt to find a more satisfactory system.   From this arose Stahl's **Phlogiston Theory,** which assumed that all combustible substances contained a principle, called **phlogiston,** which escaped in burning, and the residue was the original matter without the phlogiston it contained. This principle was always ready to combine with substances and might be transferred from one to another. For instance, lead heated lost phlogiston and became a yellow powder, the original element, but when this was heated with charcoal the latter gave up phlogiston to the powder and made it into lead.

For over a century this theory held a prominent place, and really forms the connecting link between alchemy and chemistry, for it was dominant during the transition period. Men had not yet learned to use the balance in their investigations, and to interpret its readings.

In 1774, Priestley, an Englishman, demonstrated that oxygen may be obtained from a compound of mercury by heating, and he recognized that oxygen is not phlogiston.

Lavoisier (1743-1794), one of the great scientists of the world, decided that in combustion the burning substance combines with one of the gases of the atmosphere; and that in calcining metals, as in heating mercury, this gas is taken up by the metal and may be afterwards regained.

This discovery, which Priestley missed, overthrew the phlogiston theory, dropped into the background of historical romance the last remnant of alchemy, and prepared the place for the cornerstone of chemistry which Dalton was then working at.

Lavoisier's name must always be associated with the rise of chemistry. It will also be a matter of deep regret for all time that his valuable life was ended on the guillotiné, 1794, because " The Republic had no use for men of science."

CHAPTER II.

1.—Physical and Chemical Changes.

EXPERIMENTS

1 Heat a piece of platinum wire in the flame of a spirit lamp or gas burner

Treat a piece of magnesium wire as you did the platinum.

What remains in each case?

The change in the platinum was **physical**, that in the magnesium was **chemical**.

2. Half fill a test-tube (t t) with water, boil it and hold a clean cold plate just above the mouth of the tube

Boil half an ounce of lead acetate in water until a clear solution is obtained. Hang a small piece of zinc by a thread in this solution, and let it stand for a day.

In the case of the water, what settled on the plate? Is steam a form of water?

In the case of the acetate, what was obtained? Will the substance dissolve? Hold some of it in a flame.

The water was changed physically; the acetate, chemically.

EXPLANATION.

In the case of physical change a substance may alter its state, as from solid to liquid, or may vary in some of its properties, but it remains constitutionally the same substance, neither joining with other constituents nor parting from them It may change its condition, but not its composition. Ice, water, steam are composed of precisely the same ingredients in precisely the same proportions.

When chemical change occurs there is an alteration in the constitution of the substance affected, either by giving up some of its constituents or by combining with others. The composition is always changed, the properties may be When the magnesium wire burned it formed a white ash by joining with one of the gases of the air. When the acetate of lead was brought into contact with zinc the lead separated out from the other materials as pure metal

2.—Questions and Exercises.

1. Drop a bit of limestone into some hydrochloric acid diluted one half with water What becomes of the limestone? To get an answer, evaporate some of the clear fluid, and compare the white substance left with the original limestone. Is it soluble? Has the stone become altered to something else?

2. Heat some sugar on a piece of mica or tin as long as any burning goes on. Taste the substance left. Try if it is soluble. What kind of change did the sugar undergo?

Dissolve a little of the sugar in water. Where does the sugar go? Evaporate a few drops of the solution to dryness. Compare the white substance left with the original sugar and with the residue after burning.

3.—Mixture and Combination.

EXPERIMENTS.

1. Prepare some fine iron filings, to these add about double their weight of powdered sulphur, and shake on a piece of paper until the two are thoroughly intermingled, then examine with a magnifying glass. Draw a magnet or a magnetized knife blade a number of times

through the mixture. Divide the mixture into two parts, on one drop some hydrochloric acid and carefully smell the gas that comes off. Heat the other part in a test-tube or small crucible until it glows; after cooling, again examine it with glass and magnet, then drop on it some hydrochloric acid and notice the odor of the gas formed.

2. Mix some sand and common table salt (sodium chloride), both dry, after stirring them together examine with a magnifying glass. Pour water on the mixture, stirring it meantime, and when it has stood for a few minutes filter it, evaporate the **filtrate** (that which passes through the paper), also collect what remains on the paper and dry it.

Could sand and sugar be separated in this way?

Could salt and sugar?

3. In experiment 1, were the iron and the sulphur distinguishable by mechanical processes at any time after they were put together? Would the answer be applicable during the whole treatment which they received? What evidence is there that a new substance was formed?

EXPLANATION.

A **mixture** (or mechanical mixture as it is sometimes called) is an intermingling of masses, even though very minute, of two or more substances, but each retains its own properties and identity.

If, however, the substances join together to form a third, having properties different from either of its constituents, there is said to be **combination**.

Under what conditions is it possible to separate one substance from a mixture by filtering?

A miner separates gold from sand with which it is mixed by washing; a dairyman separates milk from the sediment contained in it by straining; an engineer cleanses water from weeds, insects, and dirt in it by letting it trickle through a thick sand bed. What relation do these methods bear to the chemist's filtering?

4.—Solution.

EXPERIMENTS,

1. In a small beaker or test-tube place a little salt, then pour water on it, after standing awhile, taste the liquid by lifting a drop on the end of a piece of glass rod and placing it on the tongue.

2. Repeat this experiment using sugar instead of salt Have the salt and sugar vanished? Where are they? What state are they in?

3. Mix, in a test-tube, 1 part of sulphuric acid with 20 parts of water. Taste the mixture and say whether the acid has dissolved in the water. Repeat this experiment using equal parts of alcohol and water.

4. Fit a test-tube with a good cork and delivery tube, as in Fig. 1. Put in this tube about 2 cc. of spirits of hartshorn and invert a large dry test-tube over the mouth of the delivery tube; heat the hartshorn, and when the smell of ammonia is plainly discernible about the inverted tube, carefully place this tube, still inverted, with its mouth under water and let it stand there for a few minutes

FIG. 1.

5. Fill a large beaker with cold water from a tap or pump, let it stand unstirred in a warm room for three or four hours. The bubbles of gas on the sides of the vessel are made up of air.

How did it get there?

Where was it when the water was first put in the vessel?

Are solids soluble?

Are liquids soluble?

Are gases soluble?

EXPLANATION.

When a substance disappears in a liquid, as in the case of salt or sugar in water, it is said to **dissolve**, the liquid in which it disappears is called a **solvent**, and the resulting fluid a **solution**. The solution is **saturated** when the liquid does not take up any more of the substance; that is, when the liquid does not undergo any further change in presence of the substance. A solution is **concentrated** when it contains a relatively large portion of the dissolved substance, and it is **dilute** when the liquid is present in considerable excess.

The material dissolved takes the form of a liquid and its parts are undistinguishable from the solvent, though its presence can generally be detected, and it can be recovered unaltered in constitution or quantity, see under Chemical Change.

When a solid substance is diffused through a liquid in solid particles, as soil in muddy water, it is said to be in **suspension**. The substance here retains the solid form, though in very small masses and not evenly distributed throughout the liquid.

If there is a doubt as to whether a solid is soluble in a liquid, stir the two together, and heat, if necessary; after the solid particles settle to the bottom, lift out two or three drops of the clear liquid and *gently* evaporate this on a strip of clean glass, a bit of mica sheet, or a piece of platinum foil. If no trace of sediment is left the solid is insoluble, but if any sediment appears on the slip, it must have come from the clear fluid; hence, some of the solid was dissolved in it.

When a substance is rendered liquid through the agency of heat alone, it is said to be **fused** or **melted**, and the process is known as **fusion** or **melting**.

EXPERIMENT I.

Drop a small lump of copper sulphate into some clear water, and let it stand at rest.

From what part of the lump is matter removed?

Judging by the color, is there equal quantities of the sulphate in every portion of the liquid?

What part will become saturated first?

How is the density of water altered by dissolving a solid in it?

The solution of soluble substances is hastened by (1) powdering the solid, (2) stirring it and the solvent together, (3) suspending it in the liquid, (4) heating the liquid. Why should these operations hasten solution?

Devise an experiment to test the correctness of the last statement.

Solution is entirely a surface process, that is, it goes on at the surface where the liquid and solid are in contact How may this be demonstrated?

5.—Questions and Exercises.

1. Fill a small test-tube to the depth of 4 c. with water, and then add chloroform, or sulphuric ether, to the depth of 1 c. Shake well, and allow the mixture to stand for a few minutes. Does chloroform or ether dissolve in water?

2. Make a solution of iodine in iodide of potash solution, dilute until the color is a seal brown, then add a few drops of chloroform and shake the two together. What does this show about the relative solubility of iodine in water and in chloroform?

3. Pour about 2 cc. each of water, alcohol, sulphuric ether, chloroform, and carbon bisulphide into separate small test-tubes, then into each let fall a couple of drops of oil and shake well. Is oil soluble in any of these?

4. Where does a solid go to when dissolved? How may it be obtained from a liquid in which it is dissolved?

5. Devise means of separating salt from sand, sugar from charcoal, iodine from blacklead; in each case saving both substances.

6 Perform the following operations and decide whether the change is a physical or chemical one in each case.—

(1) Put some sugar in an evaporating dish and pour a little strong sulphuric acid on it, after standing for some hours, wash it well by turning a very light stream of water on it. Taste it

(2) Hold the end of a strip of zinc in the tip of a gas flame until it melts

(3) Take another piece of this zinc, put it in a test-tube and pour over it a little sulphuric acid diluted with twice its volume of water, after all bubbles cease to rise, evaporate the liquid.

7. How are the bubbles of gas accounted for that rise out of a bottle of soda water or of ginger ale when the cork is removed?

8. Let a little gunpowder stand in water for a few minutes, then filter it, dry the black material on the paper, and try if it will burn as the original powder does.

Does the filtrate contain a dissolved substance?

9. A blacksmith burns coal to heat iron and thus soften it. What kind of change does the coal undergo? What, the iron?

10. Are sulphur, charcoal, alum and lime soluble?

11. How does the weight of a solution compare with the weights of the solid and liquid which form it?

12. Compare the density, color, taste and smell of a solution with those of the substances that enter into it.

CHAPTER III.

1.—Conditions that Promote Chemical Change.

In some cases substances will combine chemically if simply mixed, but generally it is necessary to resort to some special treatment in order to bring about chemical combination; similarly, compounds sometimes decompose spontaneously, but in most cases the breaking up of a compound into its constituents results from methods adopted for that purpose.

The conditions that tend to promote chemical action are generally (1) either simply mixing, rubbing together, or dissolving the constituents, (2) exposing to higher temperature, (3) using electrical energy, (4) exposing to light, (5) using vital energy. Of these, solution and change of temperature are the ones more commonly employed.

2.—Intimate Mixture.

The production of chemical combination is often dependent on the bringing of the minute parts of the constituents into very near contact with each other. The methods adopted for accomplishing this result are generally (1) stirring the substances together, (2) rubbing or pounding them together, (3) mixing solutions of them.

EXPERIMENTS.

1. Wet the inside of a slightly-warmed glass beaker with strong aqua ammonia, and the inside of another beaker with a strong solution of hydrochloric acid; cover the first beaker with a glass plate, and invert it over the second. Then draw out the plate. What do the white fumes indicate? Why should they form?

2. Cut a thin slice from the end of a stick of phosphorus.* Dry it well and place on a plate, then sprinkle over it a little powdered iodine. Cover with a wide-mouthed bottle. What started the combustion?

3. In a small dish or test-tube put a piece of freshly-cut phosphorus and cover it with a strong solution of silver nitrate; let it stand for 24 hours.

Rub a little of the brown powder on a smooth glass with a knife blade.

What is it?

What did it take the place of?

4. Powder a little chlorate of potash and dry it well on a warm glass or on mica, then mix with it half its

---

* Always cut phosphorus under water, and always hold it in a pair of forceps—never in the fingers

own bulk of sulphur, by shaking them together on a piece of paper (they must not be stirred or rubbed). Place a *little* of the mixture on some hard object, such as a smooth stone or an iron plate; either strike this mixture with a hammer or rub it with a large pestle. *This experiment is dangerous unless the directions are followed.*

Where did the solid substances go?

What started the action here?

5. Mix a teaspoonful of baking soda (sodium bicarbonate, $NaHCO_3$) and half as much oxalic acid, $H_2C_2O_4$, in a large test-tube; shake them well together, then pour in a little water.

6. Dissolve a few crystals of iodide of potassium, KI, and of lead acetate, $Pb(C_2H_3O_2)_2$, in separate test-tubes, then mix the solutions. What is the rapid chemical action due to in both these cases.

3.—Heat.

Substances when heated will often undergo chemical change, both of combination and decomposition, while at ordinary temperatures they are chemically inert.

EXPERIMENTS.

1. Place about half an inch in depth of chlorate of potash, $KClO_3$, in a test-tube and heat it strongly until it melts, and bubbles of gas begin to come off, then hold in the mouth of the tube a glowing splinter. After the heating has been continued for about five minutes, allow the tube and its contents to cool, then dissolve the solid residue. At the same time make a solution of some of

the original chlorate; into each, drop a little silver nitrate solution. What do these results indicate?

2. Heat some red oxide of mercury, HgO, in a test-tube and hold a glowing splinter in the mouth of the tube.

Scrape off the grey ring that forms in the tube. What is it? Where did it come from?

EXPLANATION.

A glowing splinter that burns brilliantly, or bursts into flame, shows presence of **free oxygen.** Oxide of mercury is a combination of mercury and oxygen.

3. Make a mixture of some powdered chlorate of potash and white sugar, put a little of this on a piece of mica and heat it.

4.—Light.

EXPERIMENTS.

1. Moisten a piece of paper with nitrate of silver solution, then lay on this paper a leaf of a plant, cover the whole with a piece of glass and expose to sunlight.

2. Repeat experiment 1, but use bichromate of potash solution instead of silver nitrate.

3. Lay some opaque substance, as a coin, on a piece of blue print paper, or on a piece of photographic printing paper. Expose to the light. Note the part that was covered.

4. To some dilute solution of silver nitrate add some solution of common salt, allow the precipitate which will be formed to stand in sunlight for a time.

EXPLANATION.

A **precipitate** (ppt.) is a solid substance formed in a liquid or a mixture of liquids, and is consequently insoluble in the fluid in which it is produced.

5.—Electricity.

1. Pass a current of electricity through water in a decomposition-of-water apparatus, as in Fig. 2. This will require a current from about four bichromate cells "in series."

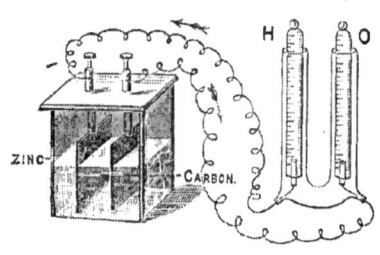

Fig. 2.

EXPLANATION.

In electrolytic decompostions those substances which are attracted to the positive electrode, or **anode** (that is the terminal attached to the copper, carbon or platinum plate), are called **electro-negative,** and those which appear at the negative electrode, or **kathode** (the terminal connected with the zinc plate), are **electro-positive.** Metallic substances are electro-positive so they always appear at the kathode.

2. Replace the water of experiment 1 by a solution of copper sulphate.

Watch the electrodes.

16 VITAL FORCE—EXERCISES

Notice if the liquid changes in depth of color When the blue color disappears, test the liquid with litmus.

Where is the copper?

6.—Vital Force.

This may not be different from the other forms of energy mentioned, but the term signifies that it is exerted by the living matter of the cells in animal and vegetable tissue

Food materials undergo chemical alterations, most of which cannot, so far, be repeated in the laboratory; some of the compounds formed being taken up as nutriment, while others are rejected as waste products.

EXPERIMENT.

1. Make a weak solution of sugar in water and add to it a little yeast powder. Let this stand for a few days in a warm place. Taste the liquid.

In this case yeast plants grow in immense numbers in the solution, using as food part of the sugar compound, while the discarded material is acid

7.—Exercises.

1. Make a mixture of powdered sulphate of iron (copperas), $FeSO_4$, and ferrocyanide of potash (yellow prussiate of potash) K_4FeCy_6 Drop some water on the mixture. What does this show?

2. A match may be lit by rubbing it against a rough surface, or by holding it against a hot object Give reasons why.

3 Powder some iodide of potash and some bichloride of mercury, then stir the two together. What indication of chemical action? Add Water

4. Rub together in a mortar a drop of mercury and a little iodine. If a drop or two of alcohol be added to dissolve the iodine, the combination will be more readily obtained. If the resultant compound is green in color, add a little more iodine; if red, add a little mercury.

5. Write your name on a sheet of white paper with a solution of sulphate of iron (copperas), when this is dry dip the paper in solution of ferrocyanide of potash. Repeat the experiment, but use tannic or gallic acid instead of the ferrocyanide. How do you explain the results?

6. Mention any industrial operations that are dependent on chemical action arising from application of heat Mention others dependent on use of light, and others on electricity.

7. Describe any domestic operations that involve the process of solution.

8. Read about the growth and nourishment of plants, and the part that light plays in the process.

CHAPTER IV.

1.—Theory of Chemical Action.

From the experiments of the last chapter, it is quite evident that two or more substances may have their parts intimately mixed with one another, yet each retain its own identity and have all its properties unchanged. In other cases, however, it is quite impossible to observe any trace of either constituent in the resultant substance, and the distinguishing properties of the kinds of matter that were acted on have been altered so that an entirely new material has been formed. It becomes necessary now to give a very brief outline of the theory which offers an explanation of this phenomenon. At the same time, it is well to warn the student that it is only a theory which at present cannot be proved; but it affords a reasonable and consistent explanation of a marvellous number of observed facts, and accounts very generally for the phenomena of chemistry

From the observation of both physical and chemical action, it is reasonably certain that all matter, of every state and condition, is made up of separated parts, very minute, indivisible by physical means, yet existing as individual portions. Such parts are called **molecules**. There are also good reasons for believing that in some forms of matter, these molecules are in rapid vibration, sometimes moving freely among one another, sometimes so confined that their vibrations may not carry them outside of a limited space.

2. In chemistry we have two kinds of matter to deal with—elementary and compound When the parts that go to make up the molecules are all of one kind, that matter is said to be elementary, because when divided or broken up as much as possible it yields only the one substance. If, however, the individual parts of the molecules are dissimilar, the substance is said to be a compound, because when properly divided up it yields matter of different kinds.

The portions of matter that go to form a molecule are called **atoms**

Chemical theory further supposes that when combination takes place the atoms of one element join with the atoms of one or more other elements to form groups of atoms, all the groups exactly alike in composition ; thus when the magnesium (Chap. II, ex. 1) burned, an atom of the metal united with an atom of oxygen, one of the gases of the atmosphere, to form a group of two atoms, *i.e*, a molecule, of oxide of magnesium, which is the chemical name of the white ash produced.

Sulphuric acid consists of two atoms of hydrogen, one of sulphur and four of oxygen (these three substances are elements). When sulphuric acid is poured on magnesium the chemical action consists in an atom of magnesium crowding out the two atoms of hydrogen that are in every molecule of the acid; this would manifestly give rise to a molecule different from that of the acid. The hydrogen is a gas, and it is the crowded-out atoms of this element congregated into masses, which form the bubbles of gas that rise to the surface. If the remaining water were evaporated a white salt would be found; this would be the matter made up of the new molecules, each composed of an atom of magnesium, one of sulphur and four of oxygen.

3. From what has been said, these statements follow:—

(1) An **atom** is the smallest part of an element that can enter into the composition of a molecule; hence, it is the unit mass that takes part in chemical action.

(2) A **molecule** is the smallest part of a substance, whether elementary or compound, that can have a separate existence.

(3) Molecules are made up of atoms; and, for the same kind of matter, their composition is constant, that is, in all molecules of the same chemical substance there are equal numbers of the same kinds of atoms.

(4) If chemical combination is the union of atoms to form molecules, then decomposition must consist, not in the separation of molecules from one another, but in the breaking of them up into atoms or into groups of atoms.

4. **Chemism.**—When masses of the same kind join together to form a single mass it is said that they **cohere**, or that they are held together by **cohesion**. When the substances that join together are of different kinds, they are said to **adhere**. When, however, atoms join together to form molecules, a new force comes into play, which is known as **chemism**, or **chemical affinity**. This differs from both cohesion and adhesion, because it is capable of acting through only infinitesimally short spaces, such as those which separate the molecules of a substance.

We have learnt in the preceding chapter that in very many instances substances will not act chemically among one another, no matter how finely they may be powdered or how intimately mixed, until means are employed to bring the molecules into still closer contact.

Chemical affinity is not equally strong among all substances. Hydrogen and chlorine can scarcely be prevented from combining if mixed, while hydrogen and nitrogen can be made to unite only with the greatest difficulty. Compounds of chlorine and nitrogen, obtained by decomposition of other substances, are held so loosely in union that they are liable to break up with violent explosions, while compounds of chlorine and iron (as well as most other metals) are very stable, that is, are not easily decomposed.

CHAPTER V

1.—Elements.

1. It has been found that by far the greater number of substances with which chemists have to deal are capable of being decomposed into simpler ones There are, however, about seventy-five substances that have never been so divided; these are called **elements**; and from them all kinds of matter have been formed, so far as we know at present. It is not likely, though, that these are all the elements, because within late years a number of new ones have been discovered. On the other hand, it is quite possible that some of those now treated as elements may be found to be compounds, when methods of research improve and a more exact knowledge of the laws of matter is gained.

2. The following list contains the names, symbols and approximate atomic weights of the more common elements. A complete list will be found in the appendix at the end of the book.

Name of Element.	Symbol.	Atomic Weight.
Aluminium	Al	27
Antimony	Sb (Stibium)	119
Arsenic	As	75
Barium	Ba	137
Bismuth	Bi	207
Boron	B	11
Bromine	Br	80
Calcium	Ca	40
Carbon	C	12
Chlorine	Cl	35·5
Chromium	Cr	52
Cobalt	Co	58·7
Copper	Cu (Cuprum)	63
Fluorine	F	19
Gold	Au (Aurum)	196
Hydrogen	H	1
Iodine	I	127
Iron	Fe (Ferrum)	56
Lead	Pb (Plumbum)	206
Magnesium	Mg	24
Manganese	Mn	55
Mercury	Hg (Hydrargyrum)	200
Nickel	Ni	58
Nitrogen	N	14
Oxygen	O	16
Phosphorus	P	31
Platinum	Pt	193
Potassium	K (Kalium)	39
Silver	Ag (Argentum)	108
Silicon	Si	28
Sodium	Na (Natrium)	23
Strontium	Sr	87
Sulphur	S	32
Tin	Sn (Stannum)	118
Zinc	Zn	65

Some of the more important ones are printed in black-face type.

2.—Metals and Non-Metals.

Elements are classified into metals and non-metals. The former are characterized by their peculiar appearance (metallic lustre), and by being good conductors of heat and of electricity. It must be remembered, however, that there is no sharp distinction between the two groups. The non-metals, in the list, are hydrogen, bromine, chlorine, iodine, fluorine, nitrogen, phosphorus, arsenic, boron, carbon, silicon, and sulphur. Arsenic serves as the connecting link between the metals and non-metals. In appearance, and, most of its physical properties, it is metallic, but chemically it is a non-metal because it does not form certain compounds which are characteristic of all true metals.

3.—Symbols.

In the column headed "Symbols," letters are placed opposite the names of the elements. These serve as a convenient, short way of indicating the substance; thus, in chemistry, H stands for hydrogen, Ca for calcium, Hg for mercury, and so on through the list. It will be noticed that in most cases the symbols are formed of the first letters of the names of the elements; or, where two or more elements begin with the same letter, the symbol is formed of the initial letter joined with one of the others that is prominently sounded in the word, thus, C stands for carbon, Ca for calcium, Cd for cadmium, and Cs for Cæsium. Generally, the names of the elements are formed after the manner of Latin nouns in "um," but in some few cases a popular name has, in ordinary use, supplanted the Latin form; though the symbol is that derived from the Latin word. Iron, copper, silver, mercury, potassium, serve as examples of this.

4.—Atomic Weights.

By atomic weight of an element is meant the number of times that an atom of the element is heavier than an atom of hydrogen. Of course, it would be absurd to think of weighing out an atom of any substance and comparing its weight with that of an atom of hydrogen. These numbers have been derived from the results of a long series of difficult experiments, which cannot be comprehended at the present stage.

Any other element might be adopted as the unit for atomic weight instead of hydrogen; but if this were done the atomic weights of all elements would be relatively changed.

CHAPTER VI.

1.—To Find out if Water is an Element.

EXPERIMENTS.

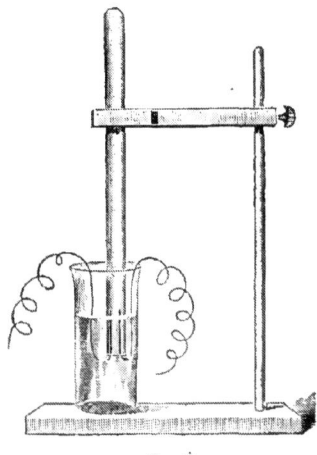

Fig. 3.

1. Take a test-tube about 2 centimetres in diameter, and 10 or 12 centimetres in length. Fill it with water mixed with a very little sulphuric acid, and invert it over a beaker containing water. Under the mouth of the test-tube, place the terminal wires of a battery, as in Fig. 3. The ends of these wires should consist of platinum, and should not touch each other when placed under the mouth of the test-tube.

2. When all the water has been expelled by the accumulated gas in the preceding experiment, raise the tube,

keeping it mouth downward, and apply a lighted match to it.

3. Repeat experiment 1, using two test-tubes full of acidulated water, inverted over a soup plate and placed side by side. Put the end of a wire under each tube. Each wire must be insulated where it touches the water, except about 1 centimetre at the end. When gas has filled one of the test-tubes, stop the current and examine the gases. Put a glowing splinter into the one with least gas in it, and apply a lighted splinter to the full one.

4. Place the battery terminals in acidulated water both in the same vessel. When the gas begins to rise freely, touch the terminals together. Why should the gas cease to rise?

5. Repeat ex. 3, but before applying the splinters turn each tube mouth upwards for a few seconds

The process of decomposing a compound by making it part of an electric circuit, is called the **Electrolysis** of it, or the *electrolytic decomposition* of it. The substance must be in the liquid state either through fusion or solution.

2 —Questions and Exercises.

1. Could the gas in the tube in experiment 1 have been produced by decomposition of the battery terminals?

2 Was the gas ordinary air? What reason for the answer? Was either gas in the next experiment air?

3. How does the mixture of gases differ from each one separately, when tested with a blazing splinter?

4. What reason for saying mixture of gases rather than the gas?

5. How many elements go to make up water?

CHAPTER VII.

1.—The Preparation and Properties of Hydrogen.

In the preceding chapter it was found that water is a compound made up of at least two substances, which physically resemble each other somewhat, but chemically are quite different. As water is one of the commonest substances known, it has been chosen as a starting point for the study of the chemical properties of matter. Of the two gases of which water is composed, the one that came off in greater quantity, and which burned when brought into the presence of a flame, is known as **hydrogen**. The methods of preparing this gas and the study of its chief properties will occupy the remainder of this chapter.

EXPERIMENTS.

1. Throw a bit of freshly-cut potassium on some water on a plate or in a wide dish. Repeat the experiment, but tinge the water red with litmus solution.

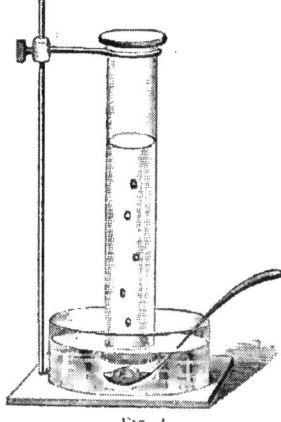
FIG. 4.

Again repeat the experiment in both ways, but use sodium instead of potassium.

2. Wrap some bits of sodium, each about half as big as a pea, in pieces of lead-sheet, such as is used in tea packages, punch some small holes through the lead, then drop it under a tube that has been inverted full of water over a dish of water, as in Fig. 4. When the sodium has disappeared,

THE PREPARATION AND PROPERTIES OF HYDROGEN. 27

another piece may be put in. (If large pieces are used a violent explosion may occur.) When the tube is filled with gas it may be lifted and a lighted taper applied to its mouth.

What state did the sodium and the potassium assume immediately after coming in contact with the water?

The sodium gradually wasted away; was the gas that came off vapor of sodium? What reasons for the answer?

3. Prepare some sodium amalgam by heating a little mercury in a test-tube to boiling, then dropping into it, in *small pieces*, one at a time, its own bulk of sodium. Hold the tube in such a way that no injury will result if burning sodium is ejected from it. When sodium enough has been added, pour the contents of the tube out on a cold plate. Put some of this under an inverted test-tube filled with water, and held mouth downwards in water.

What gas rises in the tube? Test it with a flame.

What remains of the amalgam?

Test the water with litmus.

Does the gas come from action between mercury and water? What reason for the answer?

4. Pour a little sulphuric acid into a beaker of water; fill a test-tube with this, and turn the rest out on a plate or in a glass dish. Drop a piece of zinc into the test-tube, and invert it over the plate.

Try if magnesium may be substituted for zinc?

28   THE PREPARATION AND PROPERTIES OF HYDROGEN.

Does the gas come from the action between—
- (a) Zinc and water?
- (b) Acid and water?
- (c) Zinc and acid?

What reason for the answer?

EXPLANATION.

Such chemical actions as those between sodium and water, zinc and sulphuric acid, magnesium and sulphuric acid, come under the class of **substitutions** in which one or more of the atoms of a molecule, generally the hydrogen, are displaced by atoms of other elements.

5. Fit up apparatus, as in Fig. 5. Put into the flask some zinc and water, then pour down the funnel, slowly, enough sulphuric acid to cause gas to come off freely. Collect several tubes full of gas and preserve them for future experiments.* Save the liquid in the flask, and evaporate some of it.

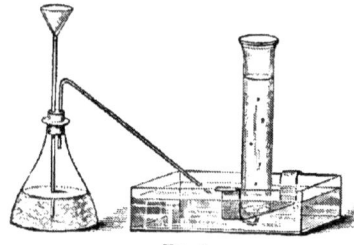

FIG. 5.

Does the zinc dissolve in the mixture of acid and water in the same sense that sugar dissolves in water?

6. Raise one of the bottles mouth downward, and pass a lighted taper upward into it. Then withdraw the taper slowly, allowing the burnt end to remain a moment or two at the mouth. Note exactly what phenomena occur,

---

*If hydrogen is to be burned, be certain that *all air* has been driven out of the generating flask and tubes. To do this allow the gas to escape for a few minutes, then collect a test-tube full over water, as in Fig. 5; bring the test-tube rapidly, mouth downwards, to a lighted lamp. If the gas burns quietly it may be collected, but if there is either a sharp explosion or a whistling sound the air is not all driven out. **Neglect to test the gas will almost certainly lead to violent and dangerous explosions.**

(1), just as the taper enters the tube (2), when the taper is inside the tube, and (3), just as it is withdrawn.

Does the gas burn?

Does it support the combustion of a candle?

Attach a piece of glass tubing drawn out fine to a gas jet. Use the glass as a burner and pass the ignited jet into a jar of hydrogen, as was done with the candle.

Does coal gas burn in hydrogen?

7. Fill two similar test-tubes with hydrogen and hold them side by side, one mouth up, the other mouth down, for a couple of minutes; then test with a lighted match to find if both are still full of the gas.

What conclusion about the relative weights of hydrogen and air?

Fill a small, light balloon with hydrogen and set it free.

8. Let a tube full of the gas stand mouth downward over water for several hours.

Does the water rise in the tube?

Is the gas soluble to any noticeable extent?

9. Prepare hydrogen gas, using the apparatus Fig. 6. Pass the gas through a tube containing fragments of calcic chloride, for the purpose of drying it; and through the cork, which should tightly fit the end of this tube, pass a glass tube drawn to a fine point. After all air has escaped apply a lighted match to the hydrogen jet.

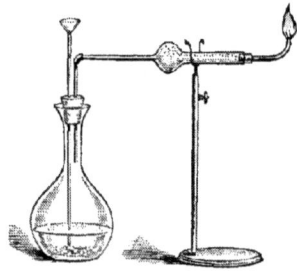

FIG. 6.

What color is the flame at first?

How does the color change?

Substitute a metal burner, such as the nozzle of a blowpipe, for the glass one.

What is the appearance of the flame now?

10. Pass a jet of burning hydrogen upward into an inverted bottle or flask that is quite dry.

What forms on the inside of the bottle?

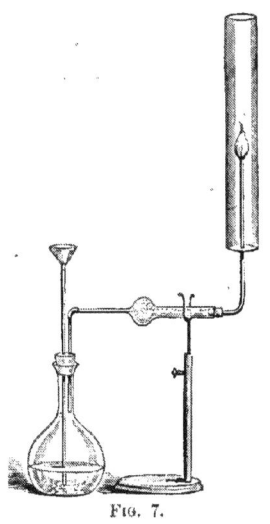

FIG. 7.

How is this material produced?

Would hydrogen that is not burning have a similar effect?

11. *The Chemical Harmonicum.*—Bring down over the jet a tube about 4 centimetres wide and 40 or 50 centimetres long, as in Fig. 7. Use tubes of different diameters and different lengths, and move them slowly up and down.

How does the flame change when the *singing* begins?

Will illuminating gas issuing from the same burner act similarly?

EXPLANATION.

The hydrogen appears to burn with a series of rapid explosions as it comes from the jet; and when the tube is of such dimensions that the air in it responds to these vibrations, the otherwise inaudible sound is increased to a distinct hum.

12. Have a vessel made out of tin or sheet-copper in the form of a double cone, as in Fig. 8. At one end,

B, have a neck for a cork, and at the other end, A, a small opening about one eighth of an inch in diameter. The vessel should be about five inches long and two and a half inches wide in the middle. Pass a hydrogen delivery tube in through B until the air and hydrogen become well mixed (or fill the vessel with oxygen and hydrogen mixed in a jar), then close B tightly with a cork, and touch the end A to a flame. Hold the apparatus so that when the cork blows out no one will be struck.

Fig 8

Why is it necessary to test hydrogen before applying a flame to it?

Why does an explosion occur here, but not in those cases in which the hydrogen issued through a jet?

2.—Questions and Exercises.

1 Make a list of the properties of hydrogen which have been observed in the preceding experiments.

2. What became of the zinc in experiment 5, and the potassium and sodium in experiment 1?

3 Mention two particulars in which the action between water and sodium differs from that between water and common salt.

4. Try if the following substances will yield hydrogen; apply heat if necessary.—

    (1) Zinc and strong sulphuric acid.
    (2) Zinc and hydrochloric acid.
    (3) Zinc and nitric acid.
    (4) Iron and hydrochloric acid.
    (5) Iron and sulphuric acid
    (6) Magnesium and sulphuric acid.

(7) Magnesium and hydrochloric acid.

(8) Copper and sulphuric acid

(9) Copper and nitric acid

(10) Aluminium and sulphuric acid

5. If a little dilute hydrochloric acid be poured on some washing soda a gas is given off, is it hydrogen?

6 If there were two jars, one full of hydrogen and the other full of air, how could you find out which jar contained each gas?

7. What reasons are there for believing that when hydrogen burns, chemical combination is going on?

EXPLANATION.

The sulphuric acid that is used with zinc for the preparation of hydrogen is diluted with four or five times its own volume of water, for two reasons. (1) The white salt, sulphate of zinc, that is formed during the chemical action is not soluble in sulphuric acid; consequently it soon covers the metal so that the acid ceases to be in contact with zinc, and the chemical action stops. Sulphate of zinc is readily soluble in water so that if the acid be made quite dilute the water dissolves the sulphate as fast as it is formed, thus permitting free action between the metal and the acid. (2) More than one chemical action is frequently possible between two substances, the particular result in any case being dependent upon such conditions as temperature and concentration. Chemical action also tends to develop heat, so that if strong acid were used, and it acted on the metal, other gases than hydrogen might be formed; for example, H_2O, SO_2, H_2S, see under Preparation of Sulphur Dioxide.

Try heating a little strong sulphuric acid up to boiling, then dropping a bit of zinc into it.

3.—Decomposition of Water by Metals.

As steam is one of the forms into which water may be changed without altering its chemical composition, any result obtained from steam by action between it and another substance is really a result of water acting on that substance.

Some metals decompose water at ordinary temperatures. Sodium and potassium are examples

EXPERIMENTS.

1. Hold a piece of sodium on a tin plate over a gas flame.

Does it fuse?

Does it change its shape?

What state is it in just before it takes fire?

2. Drop a bit of sodium on cold water.

Do the same with potassium.

What condition do the metals take when chemical action begins?

In what respects does this action resemble that of ex. 1?

How do they differ?

3 Float a piece of filtering paper on some water, then drop on this a bit of sodium; compare the result with that noticed in the last experiment.

4. Drop a piece of sodium on some water heated nearly to boiling.

What evidence of high temperature is there in these experiments?

EXPLANATION

Each molecule of water is formed of two atoms of hydrogen and one of oxygen; and one atom of the sodium or of the potassium displaces one of the atoms of the hydrogen, so that instead of the original molecule there is now a new one consisting of one atom of sodium or potassium, one atom of hydrogen and one of oxygen. The displaced atom of hydrogen escapes, and masses of these form the bubbles of gas that rise to the surface when either of these metals is sunk in water. The combustion which goes on in some of the cases when these metals float on the surface of the water, is due to the *hydrogen becoming ignited* on account of the heat generated by the rapidity of the chemical action. The different colors of the flames are owing to small portions of the metals becoming vaporized and burning along with the hydrogen.

When sodium is put on cold water, apparently there is not a sufficiently high temperature at any one place to set the hydrogen on fire, but when the metal is held still (as when on paper), or when it acts with hot water the escaping gas is ignited.

The dancing about of the globule of metal is due to the formation of gas consisting of a mixture of hydrogen and steam at the point at which the metal touches the water. This expanding gas throws the globule to one side, where the same thing happens again. A drop of water on a hot stove lid acts in a similar way for a similar reason.

5. Some metals that do not affect water at ordinary temperatures will decompose it at a red heat. Iron and magnesium are illustrations.

Experiments.

1. Take a hard glass tube about one foot in length and three quarters of an inch in diameter; fill it nearly full of clean iron filings; fit each end with a tightly-fitting cork and tube, the one leading to a pneumatic trough, the other connected with a flask containing

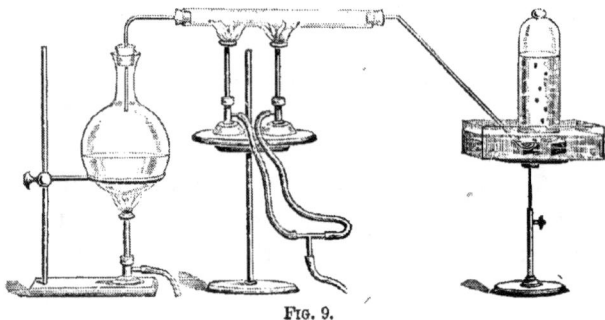

Fig. 9.

boiling water, as shown in Fig. 9. Heat the tube and filings to redness, then boil the water in the flask and force steam through the tube for some time. After the tube has cooled turn out the filings and examine them carefully. Compare with some of the original ones.

2. Collect some of the gas, prepared in the foregoing manner, and test for hydrogen, as in former experiments.

3. Repeat, but use magnesium instead of iron.

4.—Preparation of Hydrogen.

Clearly, if any element is to be obtained free from others, some substance containing that element, either in mixture or combination, must be chosen as a starting point. Not only must the material selected contain the required element, but such a decomposition and separation must be possible by the means within the operator's power as will yield the element in the condition and quantity needed

In the case of hydrogen the sources are :—

(1) Water from which the gas is set free by :
- (*a*) Electrolytic action, see experiment 3, Chap. VI.
- (*b*) Action of alkaline metals, sodium and potassium, which decompose water at ordinary temperatures.
- (*c*) Action of metals at red heat, as iron, magnesium, and lead.

(2) Acids from which hydrogen is set free by action of metals, as zinc with sulphuric acid, iron with hydrochloric acid, etc.

5—Notes on Hydrogen.

1. A gram of hydrogen at 760 mm. pressure and 0°C occupies 11 1636 (11 2 nearly) litres, hence a litre of hydrogen weighs $\frac{1}{11\,1636}=·089578$ (·0896 nearly) grams

2. The atomic weight of hydrogen is 1, its molecular weight is 2; this means that hydrogen, when freed from combination with other substances, does not continue to exist in the atomic state, but that its atoms unite in groups of at least two each. Its molecular volume is also 2, which means that each molecule occupies the space of the two atoms of which it is composed, hence there is no condensation in the change into the molecular condition

3 Hydrogen occurs chiefly in combinations such as water, the acids, the hydrides of many elements, and as a constituent of organic bodies.

4. Hydrogen, when pure, is odorless. The disagreeable smell which it has when prepared from zinc is due to impurities of the metal or acid. The chief of these are arsenic which generally causes the smell, and lead and carbon which give rise to the black flakes that float on the surface of the fluid.

5. It has already been shown that potassium and sodium decompose water at ordinary temperatures. The rarer metals barium, strontium and calcium act similarly. Vapor of water led over red-hot iron was decomposed. Zinc, nickel, tin, antimony, lead, bismuth, copper, and some other of the rarer metals will, at a red heat (1000° F.), also decompose steam.

Mercury, silver, gold and platinum do not decompose water at all.

6. Hydrogen is used to aid combustion, for reducing metallic compounds, and for filling balloons. It is one of the mixture of gases which we burn under the name of coal gas; it is freed sparingly when coal is burned in a furnace, and when water is raised to a very high temperature, especially in the presence of red-hot carbon.

CHAPTER VIII

1.—Chemical Notation.

SYMBOLS.—It was stated in a previous chapter (IV) that, very generally in chemistry, the symbols of the elements are used instead of the full names. This gives us a kind of chemical shorthand which is **brief**, expressive, and easily intelligible.

Each symbol, as used in chemical notation, stands for the name of the element, and at the same time it quantitatively represents **one atom of** that element. Thus, the symbol O stands for: (1) the name oxygen; (2) one atom of oxygen; (3) 16 parts by weight of oxygen, an atom of hydrogen being the unit of weight, usually expressed thus, ($H = 1$).

A small numeral written below and to the right of a symbol of an element indicates a molecule made up of that number of atoms, thus, O_2 is a molecule of two atoms of oxygen, S_6 is a molecule of six atoms of sulphur.

A numeral before a symbol indicates that many separate atoms, thus, $2H$ signifies two unconnected atoms of hydrogen.

2.—Formulas.

A chemical formula consists of two or more symbols, written side by side, and denotes that the elements for which the symbols stand have united to form a chemical compound. The symbol of the most electro-positive constituent of a compound, that is, the one having the most pronounced metallic properties, stands first in its formula.

When water was decomposed by electricity, the hydrogen was given off from the electrode that was connected with the *zinc*, or *negative* pole of the battery, and since oppositely electrified bodies attract each other, the hydrogen is said to be more **electro-positive** than the oxygen is.

The formula of a compound substance stands for :—
,   (1) The name of the compound ;
   (2) One molecule of the compound ,
   (3) The molecular weight of the compound.

The molecular weight is the sum of the weights of the atoms in the molecule.

A numeral placed before a formula means that number of molecules, each having the constitution indicated by the symbols in the group For example, in $4H_2O$, the 4 multiplies both the atoms and the atomic weights, and means 4 molecules, each consisting of two atoms of hydrogen and one atom of oxygen

3.—Equations.

A chemical equation consists of signs and formulas, and expresses the fact that certain substances do, of themselves, or by means of some force applied to them, re-arrange their atoms so as to form other substances of a different molecular composition.

For example, the chemical equation:—

$$H_2 + O = H_2O$$
$$\underbrace{2 + 16}\quad 18$$

expresses the fact that 2 parts by weight of hydrogen unite with 16 parts by weight of oxygen and form 18 parts by weight of water. The equation is equally true for any unit of weight, for example, that of one atom of hydrogen, one centigram, one gram, or one grain.

When two symbols or groups of symbols are connected by the sign " + ", it denotes that the substances are mixed, but not in chemical union; when symbols are written side by side without the connecting sign, the meaning is that the substances represented by them are in combination. The sign "=" is not to be understood as used in its algebraic sense of equality; it may be read "gives," or "produces," or "forms." Thus:—

$$CaCO_3 + 2HCl = CaCl_2 + H_2O + CO_2$$
$$\underbrace{100 + 73} \quad \underbrace{111 + 18 + 44}$$

may be translated: mix 100 grams (or other units) of marble with a solution of 73 grams of hydrochloric acid and they will yield 111 grams of calcic chloride, 18 grams of water, and 44 of carbonic acid gas.

The sum of all the atoms of any element on one side of the equation must equal the sum of the atoms of that same element on the other side; hence, the total number of atoms on one side equals the total number on the other, and the sum of the atomic weights on one side is identical with the sum on the other side.

4.—Classification of Chemical Actions.

For convenience of reference, chemical actions are classified as follows:—

SIMPLE COMBINATION.—When two or more substances unite to form a compound, but without causing the decomposition of any existing compound. Illustrations of this kind of change are found when magnesium burns in air, thus uniting with the oxygen to form magnesic oxide, $Mg + O = MgO$; when oxygen unites with hydrogen to form water, $2H + O = H_2O$; and when sulphur unites with iron to produce sulphide of iron, $S+Fe=FeS$.

SIMPLE DECOMPOSITION.—When a compound breaks up into simpler compounds, or into its constituent elements. Examples of this are seen when mercuric oxide decomposes into mercury and oxygen, $HgO = Hg+O$; when chlorate of potassium breaks up into oxygen and potassic chloride, $KClO_3 = KCl + 3O$.

DECOMPOSITION BY DISPLACEMENT.—When one or more of the constituents of a compound are displaced by other substances. This occurs when sodium displaces part of the hydrogen of water, $Na + H_2O = NaHO + H$; and when zinc displaces the hydrogen of sulphuric acid, $Zn + H_2SO_4 = ZnSO_4 + 2H$.

DOUBLE DISPLACEMENT.—When two compounds so act on one another that they interchange elements or groups of elements to form two new compounds. This is sometimes known as **metathesis**, and takes place in the case of potassic chloride acting on silver nitrate, $KCl + AgNO_3 = KNO_3 + AgCl$. Sodium carbonate and hydrochloric acid yield sodium chloride and carbonic acid, $Na_2CO_3 + 2HCl = 2NaCl + H_2CO_3$.

CHAPTER IX.

1.—Oxygen.

EXPERIMENTS.

1. Put a couple of grams of chlorate of potash in a test-tube, fitted with a cork and delivery tube, as in Fig. 10, then heat the tube; when bubbles of gas come off

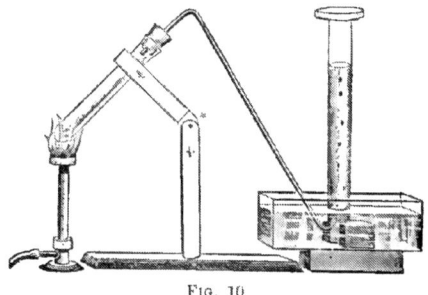

Fig. 10.

freely, hold a glowing splinter (one that is on fire but not blazing) close to the end of the delivery tube; or better, collect a tube full of the gas, as shown in the figure, and put the splinter in it. When the gas has ceased to come off, lift the delivery tube out of the water, then remove the flame from under the tube, and when the latter has cooled, dissolve the white residue; also dissolve a little chlorate of potash separately, test each with a drop of silver nitrate solution.

Does the salt undergo any change?

Upon what evidence is the answer based?

How is the gas distinguished from hydrogen, and from air?

What may be used as a test for the gas?

What physical change did the chlorate pass through?

2. Repeat the experiment, but use about a gram of red oxide of mercury instead of the chlorate. Heat until the red powder disappears.

What physical change is noticeable in the oxide?

Does oxygen come off?

Observe the grey ring in the tube, scrape a little of the deposit out on a piece of paper with a bit of wire.

What is it?

What was the substance taken?

What has been obtained from it?

What kind of chemical action went on?

3. When oxygen is wanted in quantity, it is best prepared by mixing chlorate of potash with one quarter its weight of manganese dioxide, and heating the mixture in a flask or a metal retort. The gas may be collected and stored for future use, either in a gas-holder or in suitable jars.

2.—Some Properties of Oxygen.

4. Let a tube full of the gas stand inverted over water for several hours.

Does the water perceptibly rise in the tube?

Is the gas soluble to any noticeable extent?

Does oxygen affect the color of litmus?

5. Plunge a piece of glowing charcoal into a jar of oxygen. After combustion has ceased pour a little water into the jar, and shake it well. Test with blue litmus. Add a few drops of limewater to that in the jar.

Did the oxygen burn?

Did the charcoal burn differently in oxygen from what it did in air?

What evidence is there that the gas in the jar after the charcoal burns is not oxygen?

The gas is carbon dioxide, CO_2.

6. Repeat the experiment but use sulphur instead of charcoal. A convenient means for introducing the sulphur into the oxygen is obtained by making a cup out of a bit of crayon and fitting a wire handle on it.

How is the combustion of the sulphur affected?

Is the gas formed an acid one?

Is it soluble?

The gas is sulphur dioxide, SO_2.

7. Use a shaving of phosphorus instead of sulphur. This may be easily done by screwing a chalk crayon into a nut of a small bolt so that the crayon will be upright, make a cup in its upper end for the phosphorus, and after this has been ignited lower over it a jar of oxygen. Let the mouth of the jar dip into water.

What is noticeable about the burning phosphorus?

Where do the white fumes go?

Is the gas acid?

Is the water in the jar acid?

The compound formed was phosphorus pentoxide, P_2O_5.

8. Use a piece of steel watch spring, from which the temper has been drawn, or a piece of braided picture wire, or a strand of three or four wires from a wire rope.

Heat the end of the iron, dip it in sulphur, ignite the latter, and lower it into a jar of oxygen. As the sulphur burns off, the iron should take fire.

How does it burn?

What is formed?

Examine the black oxide, Fe_3O_4.

In what respects does it differ from those products of combustion previously obtained?

9. Treat a small bit of sodium in the same way as the phosphorus in experiment 7. Again test with both blue and red litmus.

From these experiments what conclusions may be drawn with regard to :—

(1) The combustibility of oxygen;

(2) Its power of supporting combustion

Give examples of oxides that form acids in solution, and of oxides that are not acidic.

Mention an oxide that is gaseous, one that is liquid, and one that is solid at ordinary temperatures

3.—Tests for Oxygen.

1. Place a glowing splinter in oxygen; it will burn more brilliantly and will generally burst into flame

2. Fit a test-tube with cork and delivery tube, put into it some bits of copper and nitric acid, and heat gently. Collect some of the gas that comes off over water. When it becomes clear pass a little oxygen into it. The gas should turn brown and dissolve.

3. Select two test-tubes so that one will just pass mouth first into the other Fill the smaller one with

oxygen over water, and half fill the larger with a solution of pyrogallic acid mixed with some caustic potash solution Pass the smaller tube into the larger until the oxygen is in contact with the liquid, then let them stand for several hours. The liquid dissolves oxygen and turns a deep brown.

4.—Notes.

Oxygen : atomic weight, 16 ; mol. weight, 32 ; mol. vol., 2 ; density, 16.

OCCURRENCE.

Oxygen occurs free in the atmosphere, of which it forms about 21% by volume : it also exists largely in combination, for instance, it forms eight ninths of water by weight, and 48% of limestone. It is a large component of many other rocks, as silicates, phosphates, sulphates and carbonates ; and it is a constituent of most organic substances.

USES

All ordinary combustion is chemical union in which oxygen takes part, it is, therefore, necessary for the supply of heat, light and power required in domestic and industrial operations It is required for the support of animal life, and is essential for vegetable growth also.

5.—Preparation.

The sources from which oxygen gas may be derived are mostly the atmosphere, some oxides (including peroxides), some nitrates and chlorates.

It is obtained from the air through the agency of barium oxide, BaO. This, when heated to dull redness, changes into barium dioxide, BaO_2; but when heated to a somewhat higher degree it decomposes again into barium oxide and oxygen.

The more common oxides that undergo decomposition when heated, thus yielding free oxygen, are red oxide of mercury, HgO; red lead, Pb_3O_4; lead peroxide or dioxide, PbO_2; manganese dioxide, MnO_2; barium dioxide, BaO_2, and hydrogen dioxide in solution, H_2O_2.

Oxide of hydrogen, H_2O (water) yields oxygen when decomposed electrolytically.

Nitrates of potassium and sodium, when heated, decompose into the nitrites and oxygen. Chlorate of potassium also breaks up into the chloride and oxygen.

CATALYSIS.—It sometimes happens that chemical action is promoted by the presence of a substance which does not appear to take any part in the operation itself. Such a case is that of manganese dioxide in the decomposition of chlorate of potash. The chlorate breaks down at a lower temperature in the presence of the dioxide than it otherwise does, though at the end of the re-action the manganese dioxide may be recovered in the same condition and in the same quantity in which it was at the beginning. Such effects are named **catalysis** or **catalytic actions.**

It is possible that in the preparation of oxygen from chlorate of potash and manganese dioxide the latter substance may act by absorbing oxygen from the chlorate to form a higher oxide, Mn_2O_7, which on account of its instability is afterwards decomposed. There are other substances which may be substituted for the MnO_2 in this operation, viz., CuO, Fe_2O_3 and PbO. Some of these, at least, are capable of being further oxidized to CuO_2, PbO_2. (Roscoe & Schorlemmer, I, 147.)

When iron is burned in oxygen the black brittle globules that fall to the bottom are magnetic oxide of iron; they have the composition Fe_3O_4 and are generally considered to be a union of FeO_2 and Fe_2O_3, ferrous and ferric oxides respectively, hence sometimes called ferro-ferric oxide. They are similar to the "burnt iron" or black scale about a blacksmith's anvil, or the scale that forms on white-hot iron when put into water. Compare experiment 1, page 35. The red powder which settles on the side of the jar is ferric oxide, Fe_2O_3.

6.—Questions and Exercises.

1. Heat some potassium nitrate until it boils, then drop a bit of charcoal into it. What conclusion as to oxygen coming off?

2. Warm a little red lead with nitric acid. The brown powder is lead dioxide, PbO_2. Separate it from the liquid, dry it, and try if it will yield oxygen when heated. What is left after heating?

3. How may oxygen be separated from a mixture of which it is one ingredient?

4. Using the chalk cup of experiment 7, page 44, to hold a freshly-cut shaving of phosphorus, place a gas jar or bottle filled with air over it so that the mouth of the jar dips into water, let it stand for a day. The small wreaths of smoke that are noticed rising from the phosphorus when first cut are composed of the same oxide that was produced when phosphorus burned in oxygen. Devise a way of adapting this experiment to measuring the proportion of oxygen in air.

5. Make a list of the properties of oxygen that have been observed. In what particulars does it resemble air?

6. From what compounds has oxygen been obtained in the experiments so far? What elements have combined with oxygen, and what compounds have they formed? Are any of these compounds of common occurrence?

7. Hydrogen burns in air, should it burn in oxygen also?

8. Refer to any experiment that supports the answer given.

CHAPTER X

Oxidation and Reduction.

EXPLANATION.

When a substance unites chemically with oxygen, the process is called **oxidation**. Chemists use that term, however, in a somewhat wider sense to indicate union with the non-metallic element of a molecule, thus, when $FeCl_2$ changes to $FeCl_3$, it is described as oxidation. Similarly, if As_2S_3 altered to As_2S_5 it would be said to oxidize from the trisulphide to the pentasulphide. It will be sufficient for the purposes of this book to understand the term as denoting union with oxygen. The experiments of the previous chapter are mostly illustrative of this operation.

The opposite process is known as **reduction**, and consists of the withdrawal of one or more of the **electro-negative** (non-metallic) elements or radicals from the molecular group.

When $Fe(NO_3)_3$ is altered to $Fe(NO_3)_2$ it is said to be reduced from ferric to ferrous nitrate. Similarly, PbO_2 may be reduced first to PbO and finally to metallic lead.

The following experiments illustrate these changes:—

EXPERIMENT I.

Put a mixture of red lead and powdered charcoal into a hard glass tube closed at one end, put some pieces of chalk loosely in the open end to prevent free access of air, then heat the mixture strongly. What remains?

What became of the charcoal?

OXIDATION AND REDUCTION.

When charcoal burns it unites with oxygen to form CO or CO_2. Where did the oxygen come from to support the combustion?

What took place in the way of oxidation and of deoxidation?

2. Take a hard glass tube, drawn out fine, and place in it a small quantity of black oxide of copper. Connect it with a tightly-fitting cork and tube to a hydrogen

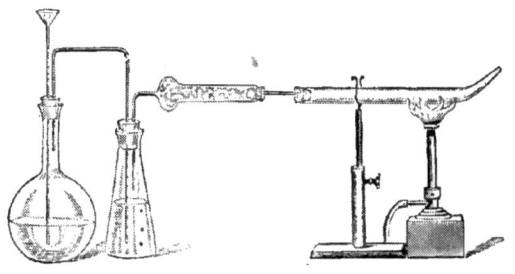

Fig. 11.

generating apparatus. The gas must be dried by passing it through calcic chloride or sulphuric acid, before it reaches the tube with the oxide of copper in it. (See Fig. 11.) After allowing the hydrogen to escape for a few minutes, *so as to drive out all the air* from the apparatus, heat the oxide of copper. Condensed vapor of water should pass out of the point of the tube.

What change of color is there in the copper oxide?

What remains in the tube?

This is a case both of oxidation and reduction; explain.

Will hydrogen alone take oxygen away from copper?

Will heating in a gas flame decompose the oxide and leave metallic copper?

Heat a little of the red copper powder on a piece of mica, in the tip of a flame, where it will be exposed to air.

3. Repeat the experiment, but use red iron rust, Fe_2O_3, instead of copper oxide. Grind the rust to fine powder in a mortar before putting it in the tube.

4. Will red lead, Pb_3O_4, yield similar results?

5. Using a small tube, heat a little silver nitrate in a current of hydrogen. Hold a bit of blue litmus paper at the outlet of the tube When the action is completed break the tube and examine what is left of the nitrate.

Questions.

1. Mention cases in which heat alone will cause reduction of a compound.

2. Explain the action of carbon and hydrogen in reducing the oxides of copper and iron.

3. Houses are sometimes heated by hot water. In such cases if the air-vent of the uppermost radiators be opened after the furnace has been burning for some time, a considerable volume of gas will frequently escape, and if a lighted match be held to this gas it will burn readily How may its formation be accounted for? Refer to experiment 1, page 35.

What reduction went on?

Read about smelting iron ores.

CHAPTER XI.

Hydrogen Dioxide or Peroxide.

Usually when a peroxide of a metal is treated with an acid the same salt is formed that would be produced from the normal oxide, and one atom of oxygen is set free, thus :—$PbO_2 + H_2SO_4 = PbSO_4 + H_2O + O$. In the case of barium dioxide the atom of oxygen is not at once liberated, but goes to form another oxide of hydrogen, H_2O_2, thus:—$BaO_2 + H_2SO_4 = BaSO_4 + H_2O_2$. Hydrogen dioxide is an unstable substance that can be kept only in solution, if it is driven off from the water in which it is formed it decomposes into H_2O and O.

EXPERIMENTS.

1. Treat some barium peroxide, BaO_2, with some sulphuric acid, and when the precipitate ceases to form, filter. The filtrate is a solution of hydrogen dioxide.

Prepare some test-paper as follows:—Boil some starch to a paste, drop into it a little potassic iodide, dip in this strips of white unsized paper (strips from a leaf of a scribbler will answer).

Let a drop of the liquid filtrate fall on this paper. The bluing is due to oxygen displacing the iodine from its union with potassium and the free iodine combining with the starch.

2. Make solutions of logwood, indigo, litmus, permanganate of potash (acid), and aniline blue, separately. Add some solution of hydrogen dioxide to each and let them stand.

The results are due to oxidation of the coloring matter, such a change in composition alters the characteristic color of the original substance.

3. Hang a piece of the test-paper in a test-tube above some H_2O_2, then evaporate the latter by heating

4. Make a solution of lead acetate in boiling water, add to this some solution of hydrogen sulphide. Let the black precipitate (lead sulphide) settle to the bottom, pour off the clear liquid and add hydrogen dioxide solution. The formation of a white powder shows oxidation of the sulphide to sulphate.

5 Repeat the experiment, but use iodide of potash solution for hydrogen sulphide

EXPLANATION.

The chemical action of hydrogen peroxide is due to the weak chemical attraction existing between one of the oxygen atoms and the other parts of the molecule, that is, H_2O. Whatever may be the molecular structure of the group of atoms, it is clear from the result of its decomposition that one atom of oxygen is held very loosely, hence easily breaks away from the others as an atom. These loose atoms join with any substance present that has an attraction for oxygen.

USES.

Hydrogen dioxide is used as a bleaching agent, and for purposes of oxidation in chemical work. In acid solution it may be kept fairly well for a time without decomposition.

CHAPTER XII.

Ozone.

When an electric machine is worked in dry air a peculiar odor is noticeable in the neighborhood of the plates, which becomes more distinct as sparks pass between the terminals. This is due to the formation of **ozone** from the oxygen of the air. The substance known as ozone is neither a combination of oxygen with other matter, nor is it a decomposition of that gas, but is produced by a re-grouping of the atoms in the molecules. Under ordinary conditions the atoms of oxygen, when set free from combinations, unite in groups of two, thus, the molecular symbol is O_2 or $O=O$; but in special circumstances the grouping seems to be in threes, thus, O_3 or $\overset{O-O}{\underset{O}{\diagdown\diagup}}$ and this modification makes oxygen into ozone.

EXPERIMENTS.

1. Hang a stick of freshly scraped phosphorus in a large bottle with a little water in the bottom of it. After some hours smell the gas in the bottle, and test it with iodized starch paper, as used for hydrogen dioxide.

Dip a strip of red litmus paper in iodide of potash solution and hang it in the bottle.

2. Pour a little dilute sulphuric acid on undissolved barium dioxide. Use the same test-papers for the gas that comes off.

"Ozone is formed during the oxidation of phosphorus by free oxygen . . . . . . and by the action of sulphuric acid on barium dioxide, potassium permanganate and other substances which evolve oxygen in the cold on being thus treated" Ramsay, 388.

Explanation.

Ozone is an **allotropic** form of oxygen. This term is applied to elements that have chemically the same composition, but on account of different molecular groupings have some properties that are not alike. Other instances of allotropism will be met with under carbon, sulphur and phosphorus.

It is not possible, by any known means, to convert a volume of oxygen entirely into ozone unless the latter gas is absorbed by turpentine or ether as fast as formed. In accordance with the molecular law of volumes (page 75) there is a contraction in the volume of oxygen as it alters to ozone, and an expansion in the reverse process.

Ozone is an unstable substance that decomposes into oxygen according to the equation $2O_3 = 3O_2$, or $2O_2O = 3O_2$. Because of this ready freeing of oxygen in the atomic condition ozone is an active oxidizing agent in the laboratory.

Occurrence.

Ozone is found in small quantities in the atmosphere, more abundantly though after electric storms, and in the neighborhood of the ocean and of pine forests.

CHAPTER XIII.

Nascent State.

Many substances, particularly elements, at the instant at which they are freed from combination, possess a chemical activity which requires a special explanation

Ordinary oxygen does not bleach indigo, logwood, litmus or permanganate of potash solutions, yet ozone, which is only oxygen in a somewhat altered molecular combination, does destroy the colors of these substances. So does the oxygen set free by decomposing hydrogen dioxide.

Hydrogen gas may be led for days through silver chloride, held in suspension in water, yet the chloride will not be decomposed. If, however, some silver chloride (prepared by dropping hydrochloric acid, or a solution of a chloride, into a solution of silver nitrate) be spread on a piece of zinc and the whole immersed in dilute sulphuric acid, the silver chloride will, in a few hours, be reduced to metallic silver, (1) $Zn + H_2SO_4 = ZnSO_4 + 2H$. (2) $H + AgCl = HCl + Ag$. Similarly, a current of hydrogen passed through potassic chlorate solution has no effect on it, but hydrogen generated in the solution from some pieces of zinc and dilute sulphuric acid will reduce the chlorate to the chloride of potassium, $Zn + H_2SO_4 = ZnSO_4 + 2H$, and $6H + KClO_3 = KCl + 3H_2O$. Free hydrogen has no effect on nitric acid, but hydrogen freed from a compound in presence of the acid at once reduces it, (1) $Zn + 2HNO_3 = Zn(NO_3)_2 + 2H$. (2) $2H + 2HNO_3 = 2H_2O + 2NO_2$. This is the reason that zinc and nitric acid do not yield free hydrogen but an oxide of nitrogen generally. Many substances in solution are oxidized by passing chlorine gas through the liquid. Now chlorine contains no oxygen, so we are obliged to look elsewhere for a reason for this change. It is well known that chlorine has a great affinity for hydrogen; so strong indeed is this attraction, that it breaks up the water molecules, appropriates the hydrogen for the formation of hydrochloric acid, and sets the oxygen free, and it is this latter which oxidizes the substances, $2Cl + H_2O = 2HCl + O$, though a stream of oxygen gas produces no such effect. Numerous instances might be given of similar chemical action brought about by elements at the instant at which they are freed from combination, though they do not retain the power for any appreciable length of time. When the molecule of a compound is decomposed, the constituents pass off as atoms, and these may either unite with other elements to form new combinations, or may remain uncombined with any other substance; but in the latter case they join with each other, and, since the combining powers of atoms are limited, in amount, though for different elements these amounts are different, it follows that if two atoms of the same kind combine with each other their affinity for other atoms is lessened by the amount of attraction by which they are held together. Their chemical activity in the way of forming new combinations will, therefore, be reduced; hence, at the instant at which atoms are freed from molecules and exist as individual atoms, their chemical attraction for other atoms is stronger than it is after they have joined in groups. ❲ At the time at which a portion of an element exists as atoms, and before these have united to form molecules, it is said to be in the

nascent state.) When the molecule of ozone breaks up into a molecule of oxygen and an atom of oxygen, the latter is in the nascent condition, that is, uncombined with any other atom, so that its powers of combination are not impaired in any way. On this account it oxidizes, and thus destroys the coloring matters spoken of; and decomposes potassic iodide by oxidizing the potassium, $O_3 + 2KI = O_2 + K_2O + I_2$. Similarly the hydrogen atoms when first liberated decompose silver chloride, reduce nitric acid, reduce potassic chlorate and decompose sulphuric acid under proper conditions. The *nascent* oxygen resulting from the spontaneous decomposition of the hydrogen peroxide molecule, or from the action of chlorine on the water molecule, acts in a way precisely similar to that in which the oxygen does, when the ozone molecule is broken up. The chemical activity of elements in the nascent condition is a most important factor in some industrial operations, notably the bleaching of fibres and pulp, and in oxidation and reduction processes.

CHAPTER XIV.

Acids, Bases and Salts.

1. It has been necessary several times to mention substances which have been called **acids**. These form one of three classes that include a great many chemical compounds. The other two are **bases** and **salts**. Salts and acids are always compounds; bases also are compounds, being hydroxides of metals. Oxides and hydroxides of the non-metals are generally acid-forming, and those of the metals are mostly basic.

ACIDS. 59

Hydroxides or **hydrates** are compounds formed by the union of an atom of an element with one or more hydroxyl radicals, (HO), thus KHO, $Mg(HO)_2$, $Ca(HO)_2$. Such hydrates often result from the union of the oxide with water, thus $CaO + H_2O = Ca(HO)_2$. Water itself may be considered a hydroxide of hydrogen, $H(OH)$. Sodium will replace the hydrogen atom in this group to form sodium hydroxide, $NaHO$.

2.—Acids.

In order to learn some of the general properties of acids, perform the following experiments, using nitric, hydrochloric, sulphuric, acetic, tartaric, oxalic, and citric acids.

1. Pour some of the acid, or drop a crystal about as big as a pea if the acid is a solid, into twenty or thirty times its own volume of water in a test-tube. Taste the solution

2. Half-fill a small test-tube with blue litmus solution and add to it some of the diluted acid Add some of the acid to some red litmus solution also.

3. Place some "bread soda," bicarbonate of sodium, $NaHCO_3$, in a test-tube, and pour some of the dilute acid upon it.

Tabulate the results as follows —

Name of Acid	Taste	Action on Red Litmus	Action on Blue Litmus	Action on Bread Soda	REMARKS

All acids contain replaceable hydrogen in the molecule; that is, hydrogen which may be driven out by one or more atoms of some other substance. A familiar example is in the preparation of hydrogen gas from sulphuric acid, in which two hydrogen atoms are replaced by one of zinc.

3.—Bases.

Any metallic hydroxide, the metal of which is capable of replacing the hydrogen of an acid is a **base**. The hydrogen of acids may also be replaced by metals, the term base, however, is usually applied only to the hydrates. A molecule of an hydroxide is formed by the union of a metallic atom with one or more hydroxyl groups, (HO). Examples of these have already been met with when potassium and sodium were thrown on water. Hydrates are formed either by direct action of the metal on water (this occurs only with some of the alkalies) or by dissolving the oxide in water. (There is a third method which need not be discussed here, as it belongs essentially to the chemistry of the metals.)

EXPERIMENTS.

1. Take a piece of the metal potassium, about the size of a pea, place it in an iron spoon, and heat it over a spirit lamp until it has ceased to burn. Then add a little water, and test the solution with red, and with blue litmus, and with turmeric paper. Taste the solution after diluting it largely.

2. Repeat this experiment, using the metals, magnesium and sodium. Evaporate some of the solution.

The substances formed are hydroxides of the metals.

4 —Salts.

When the hydrogen of an acid is replaced by a metal, or the metal of a base, the resulting compound is a **salt**.

EXPERIMENTS.

1. Take a little of the sodium compound from the last experiment, and dissolve it completely in a test-tube of water, then add to it hydrochloric acid, drop by drop, until it is neutralized, pour half of this solution into an evaporating dish, place on a sand bath and heat until all the water is driven off. Carefully examine the residue. Taste it. Is it caustic soda?

Pour the rest of the solution into a flat dish of any kind, and allow it to remain for a day or two in a warm room.

2. Potassium hydroxide, slaked lime (calcium hydroxide), and magnesium hydroxide may be used as other examples of bases. When treated with acids they form salts.

5.—Basicity of Acids.

Acids in which there is one replaceable hydrogen atom in each molecule are **monobasic**. Nitric, hydrochloric and acetic acids are examples. These have the formulas HNO_3, HCl, $HC_2H_3O_2$ respectively. Those acids in which there are two atoms of replaceable hydrogen in the molecule are **dibasic**. Sulphuric acid, H_2SO_4, carbonic acid, H_2CO_3, and oxalic acid, $H_2C_2O_4$, are examples.

Acids with three atoms of replaceable hydrogen in the molecule are **tribasic**. Phosphoric acid, H_3PO_4, is an example of this class.

CHAPTER XV.

Chemical Nomenclature.

Chemical names doubtless appear bewildering in their variety, but a few simple principles underlie their use, and once these are mastered, there will be little difficulty in elementary chemistry, in fitting the proper name to a formula or giving the composition of a substance, once the name is known.

I.

Binary compounds, that is, those of two elements, have names that end in -ide. The most electro-positive element stands first (which one this is, will be learned by practice), and its name may be in either the noun or adjectival form in the complete designation. Thus KCl is potassic chloride, potassium chloride or chloride of potassium; H_2S is hydric sulphide, hydrogen sulphide or sulphide of hydrogen.

II.

When the electro-negative element unites in more than one proportion with the other, the number of parts of it in any particular combination are indicated by the prefixes **mono** or **mon-**, **di-**, **tri-**, **tetr**, or **tetra-**, and **pent-**. Thus H_2O (water) is chemically hydrogen monoxide; H_2O_2 is hydrogen dioxide; CO is monoxide of carbon; CO_2 is carbon dioxide; PCl_3 is phosphorus trichloride; CCl_4 is carbon tetrachloride; P_2O_5 is phosphorus pentoxide. An old ending, **-uret**, is sometimes used instead of **-ide**, and **prot-** is an old prefix used instead of **mono-**.

III.

In the names of acids the endings **-ous** and **-ic** very generally occur, and they indicate that the acid whose name ends in **-ic** has in its composition a greater quantity of oxygen than the one whose name ends in **-ous**. This does not mean that either of these endings points to a fixed number of atoms of oxygen in the molecule, but that relatively the -ous acid always has in it less oxygen than the -ic acid. Thus HNO_3 is nitric acid, and HNO_2 nitrous acid; $HClO_2$ chlorous acid, $HClO_3$ chloric acid; H_2SO_3 sulphurous acid, and H_2SO_4 sulphuric acid. The prefixes **hypo** (beneath) and **per** (above) are used also with regard to the quantity of oxygen in the molecule of the acid. Thus $HClO$ is hypochlorous acid, $HClO_2$, chlorous acid; $HClO_3$, chloric acid, and $HClO_4$ perchloric acid. Hypochlorous means, then, below chlorous as regards the number of atoms of oxygen in the molecule, and perchloric is above chloric in the same respect.

IV.

In naming salts the prefixes belonging to the names of the acids are preserved, but in the name of the salt the ending **-ous** of the acid is changed into **-ite**, and the ending **ic-** of the acid into **-ate** Thus $KClO$ is hypochlorite of potassium; $NaClO_2$ chlorite of sodium; $AgClO_3$ chlorate of silver, and $KClO_4$ perchlorate of potassium; $CaSO_4$ is sulphate of calcium, and $Cu(NO_2)_2$ is nitrite of copper. In salts the adjectival form of the name of the base may be used. Thus $AgSO_3$ is argentic sulphite, or silver sulphite, or sulphite of silver; KNO_3 is potassic nitrate, potassium nitrate, or nitrate of potassium.

CHAPTER XVI.

1.—Valency.

The student who has followed this book thus far will probably have had some difficulty in deciding in what proportions elements unite with one another. The object of this chapter is to explain this difficulty, as far as can be done at this elementary stage.

The following are the formulas of some well-known compounds :—

$HCl, H_2O, NH_3, CH_4 ; KCl, FeCl_2, PCl_3, CCl_4.$

In the first four, hydrogen unites in proportions of one, two, three and four atoms with one atom respectively of chlorine, oxygen, nitrogen and carbon. The second group shows similar compounds of chlorine. It seems, therefore, that one atom of hydrogen unites with one atom of chlorine to form a definite stable compound, while it takes two atoms of hydrogen to form such a compound with one of oxygen, three atoms of hydrogen with one of nitrogen, and four of hydrogen with one of carbon. Just as the atom of hydrogen is taken as the unit of atomic weight, so it is taken as the unit of combining power and the other elements are *valued* with reference to this one. Thus an element, one atom of which unites with one atom of hydrogen, or replaces an atom of hydrogen in combination is said to be a **univalent** or a **monad** element, that is, it is worth one. Similarly an element, one of whose atoms is capable of uniting with two atoms of hydrogen, or of replacing two atoms of hydrogen in a compound, is called a **bivalent** or **diad** element—worth two. For instance, in the combination HCl chlorine is a monad because one atom of it unites to form a stable compound with one atom of hydrogen. Similarly in the equation $KHO + HCl = KCl + H_2O$, one atom of potassium replaces one atom of hydrogen, hence the metal has a valency of one. Sulphur and zinc are diads in the following combinations: $FeS + 2HCl = FeCl_2 + H_2S$, and $Zn + H_2SO_4 = ZnSO_4 + 2H$.

According to this classification elements are divided into **monad** or **univalent**, **diad** or **bivalent**, **triad** or **trivalent**, **tetrad** or **tetravalent**, **pentad** or **quinquivalent**, and **hexad** or **hexevalent** elements. The combining value of an atom of an element, or its replacing power, in terms of the number of atoms of hydrogen with which it unites or which it displaces, is known as its **valency**. Even for the same element this valency is frequently a variable quantity. The reasons for this cannot be considered until a later stage, but a few examples will make clear its importance. H_2O and H_2O_2 are both compounds of hydrogen and oxygen; sulphur and oxygen form SO_2 and SO_3, carbon and oxygen unite to produce the oxides CO and CO_2; FeO, Fe_2O_3 and Fe_3O_4 are three oxides of iron; and of lead and oxygen we have the compounds PbO, Pb_2O_3, Pb_3O_4 and PbO_2.

Substances of equal valency unite in proportion of one to one, others in such proportion that the valencies of the atoms or radicals of one kind equal those of the atoms of the other kind in the molecule

If there are six elements whose valencies are indicated by the Roman numerals (the common way of marking it), and whose names are represented by letters, thus,

A^i, B^{ii}, C^{iii}, D^{iv}, E^v, F^{vi}, they may form combinations as follows: A_2B, A_3C, A_4D; C_2B_3, B_2D, E_2B_5, B_3F, D_3C_4, etc.

It must not be inferred from what is said above that every element is capable of uniting with every other one. There are many cases in which two elements have never been known to unite directly with each other, or to form a group from the breaking down of higher compounds; examples are, oxygen and fluorine, potassium and sodium, hydrogen and bismuth.

2.

The following table gives the valency of the principal elements:—

	MONADS.	DIADS.	TRIADS.	TETRADS.	PENTADS.	HEXADS.
NON-METALS.	Bromine. Chlorine. Fluorine. Hydrogen. Iodine.	Oxygen. Sulphur.	Boron. Nitrogen. Phosphorus. Arsenic.	Carbon. Silicon. Sulphur.	Nitrogen. Phosphorus. Arsenic.	Sulphur.
METALS.	Potassium. Sodium. Silver.	Calcium. Copper. Magnesium. Mercury. Manganese. Strontium. Zinc. Iron. Barium. Lead.	Antimony. Bismuth. Gold. Aluminium.	Cobalt. Iron. Lead. Manganese. Nickel. Platinum. Tin.	Antimony. Bismuth.	Chromium. Manganese. Iron.

Many of the elements do not unite directly with hydrogen; when this is the case their valencies are calculated from their union with other elements whose combinations with hydrogen are known.

3.—Radicals.

In many cases a group of atoms acts in combination and replacement in the same way that single atoms do. An example of this we have already met in the hydroxyl group HO, which unites with potassium and sodium to form the hydrates of these metals.

$$K + H_2O + = KHO + H.$$

These *radicals*, as they are called, do not exist in the free state, but when separated in the decomposition of compounds, they unite either with each other or with some other substance present.

That part of the molecule which remains when the hydrogen is taken away in the case of an acid is called the **acid radical.** It forms part of the molecule in both the acid and the salt. Thus, NO_3 is the radical of nitric and SO_4 of sulphuric acid. This radical is monad, diad, or triad, depending on whether it is joined with one, two or three atoms of hydrogen in the acid.

4.—Replacement of Hydrogen in Acids.

The atoms of hydrogen in an acid molecule are replaceable, one by one, by the atoms of a monad metal In the case of a monobasic acid, therefore, only one series of salts occurs, thus :—

$$HNO_3 + K = KNO_3 + H$$
$$2HNO_3 + Cu = Cu(NO_3)_2 + 2H.$$

Since copper is a diad it replaces two and only two atoms of hydrogen, and to secure these two atoms two molecules of the acid must be taken.

With a dibasic acid, as H_2CO_3, and a monad base, two series of salts are formed:—

thus $H_2SO_4 + K = KHSO_4 + H$,
and $KHSO_4 + K = K_2SO_4 + H$,
or $H_2SO_4 + 2K = K_2SO_4 + 2H$.

Of course such salts are possible only when the valency of the base is less than the **basicity** of the acid;—the basicity being determined by the number of atoms of replaceable hydrogen in the molecule.

Those salts which have replaceable hydrogen in the molecule are called **acid salts**; those in which all the hydrogen is replaced are **neutral**.

In the case of a tribasic acid, one, two, or three of its hydrogen atoms may be displaced, and these not necessarily by the same base, thus:—

H_3PO_4 is tribasic phosphoric acid;

NaH_2PO_4 is sodium di-hydrogen phosphate;

Na_2HPO_4 is di-sodium hydrogen phosphate;

Na_3PO_4 is neutral sodium phosphate;

$NaNH_4HPO_4$ is sodium ammonium hydrogen phosphate.

Such a salt as $NaHCO_3$ is named either acid carbonate of sodium, sodium hydrogen carbonate, or bi-carbonate of sodium.

5.—Equivalent.

Chemical Equivalent is a term used to express the proportions, by weight, in which elements combine with one another, or displace one another in a compound, one part, by weight, of hydrogen being taken as a unit. Thus, the chemical equivalents of oxygen, sulphur, chlorine and nitrogen from the compounds H_2O, H_2S, HCl and NH_3, are, respectively, 8, 16, 35·5, 4·66.

Chemical equivalents must not be confounded with combining proportions. The former are taken with reference to hydrogen only; the latter may be taken with reference to any other element. Thus from CH_4 we get the equivalent of carbon, but from CO, and CO_2, are obtained the two proportions in which carbon and oxygen combine.

6.—Questions and Exercises.

1. Given the acids HNO_3, H_2CO_3, and copper, potassium, sodium hydrate and silver, write the formulas for all the salts that theoretically could be formed. Write the names of these salts.

2. Which one out of each of the following pairs is correct and why? (1) $PbNO_3$ or $Pb(NO_3)_2$; (2) $ZnHSO_4$ or $ZnSO_4$; (3) $NaSO_4$ or $NaHSO_4$, (4) $AgSO_4$ or Ag_2SO_4.

3. From what acid is each of the following prepared, and what is its basicity, as shown by the salt? KNO_2, $Pb(NO_2)_2$, Na_2SO_3, $CaSO_4$, $Ba(NO_3)_2$.

4. Why is the compound whose formula is $KHSO_4$ called a sulphate?

Why is it an acid sulphate? Why is it acid sulphate of potassium?

5. Considering the two compounds $KHSO_4$ and K_2SO_4 why should the former be named bi-sulphate?

6. Write formulas for nitrate of calcium, sulphate of sodium, zinc chloride, silver sulphite, silver sulphide, silver carbonate.

7. Give names to the substances for which the following are the formulas:—

CaO, $Ca(HO)_2$, $BaCl_2$, $Ba(NO_3)_2$, $BaCO_3$, $ZnCO_3$, K_2CO_3, $NaHCO_3$, $FeCO_3$, K_2SO_3, Ag_2S, PbS.

8. The following formulas are correctly written. Explain the difference between the members of each pair:—

$NaCl$, $CaCl_2$; $AgNo_3$, $Pb(NO_3)_2$; K_2SO_4, $CuSO_4$; FeS, CS_2 ; BaO, SO_2 ; KHO, $Ca(HO)_2$; Ag_2CO_3, $MgCO_3$.

9. "In its -ic compounds, sulphur is a hexad." What is the meaning of this statement? What would be the formula for the oxide under these conditions?

10. What determines the valency of an element? What the basicity of an acid?

CHAPTER XVII.

1.—Synthesis of Water.

A compound is said to be **analyzed** when it is separated into its constituents and these determined. Analysis may be of two kinds,—**qualitative**, when the operator simply finds what the constituents are; **quantitative**, when he goes further and calculates the proportions by weight or volume in which these constituents enter into the compound. The opposite of analysis is **synthesis.** This consists in bringing together the components and treating them in such a way that they unite to form the compound required. When water was decomposed by electricity, and it was shown that hydrogen and oxygen were the constituents (page 25), we had a qualitative analysis of it; on the other hand, when oxygen and hydrogen are caused to unite, and it is shown that water is the result of the union, we have a synthesis of it.

EXPERIMENTS.

1. Burn a jet of hydrogen in an inverted bottle. What is produced?

2. Fill a eudiometer with mercury and invert it over a dish of mercury, Fig. 12. Lead into it 10 cc. of hydrogen

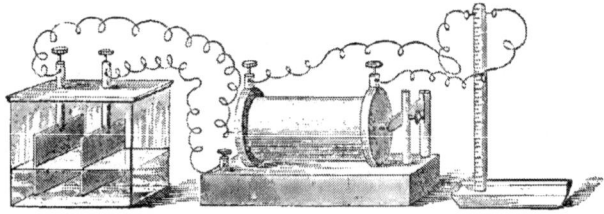

Fig. 12.

and 5 of oxygen, pass a spark between the wire points. What happens?

Examine the top of the tube carefully for moisture.

3. Fill a dry test-tube over mercury with a mixture of hydrogen and oxygen, two parts of the former to one of the latter, hold the mouth of the tube to a flame; after the explosion see if there is moisture inside the tube.

4. Repeat experiment 2, using equal portions of hydrogen and oxygen.

Test the gas that remains by adding hydrogen and again passing the spark between points.

5. Show the relation of experiment 1, page 35, and experiment 2, page 50, to the composition of water.

6. In this use of the eudiometer what purpose does the electric spark serve?

Would a flame do as well?

Could a flame be applied to the gases in the tube?

7. What volumes of hydrogen and oxygen will combine to form water?

From these volumes, calculate the weights of hydrogen and oxygen that combine to form water.

2.—Composition of Steam by Volume.

Since two volumes of hydrogen combine with one of oxygen to make water vapor, a natural conclusion would be that if the vapor were not allowed to condense there would be three volumes of it. This problem has now to be experimentally determined.

EXPERIMENT.

Pass into a eudiometer about 12 cc. of a mixture of hydrogen and oxygen gases—using two volumes of the former to one of the latter. Cover the eudiometer with a large tube, into the top and bottom which pass tightly-fitting corks perforated with tubes, admitting steam at the top from the flask on the left, and giving exit to it at the bottom, Fig. 13. The wires from the battery to the eudiometer should pass into the jacket through its upper cork. After the steam has been admitted mark the height of the mercury above that in the trough, and also the volume of the contained gases, then explode them. After explosion depress the eudiometer, until the mercury in the tube stands the same height above that in the trough as before. Then measure the volume of the water-gas (steam) in the eudiometer, and compare this volume with that of the original mixture.

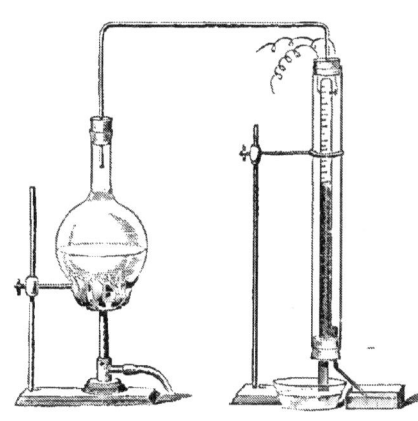

FIG. 13.

If we represent equal volumes of oxygen and of hydrogen by equal squares, and then place in these squares the first letter of the name of these elements, we can represent to the eye, by another figure, the volume of water-gas or steam formed, and the diminution in volume which occurs after union. Thus :—

$$\left.\begin{array}{c}\boxed{\begin{array}{c}1\text{ vol.}\\ H\end{array}}\\ \boxed{\begin{array}{c}1\text{ vol.}\\ H\end{array}}\end{array}\right\} + \boxed{\begin{array}{c}1\text{ vol}\\ O\end{array}} = \boxed{\begin{array}{c}2\text{ vols}\\ \text{steam}\end{array}}$$

Similar experiments with other substances in the gaseous condition show that in some cases there is no change of volume, while in some there is an increase, and in others a diminution. These do not occur at random, however, as the following considerations will show.

3.—Avogadro's Law.

Gaseous bodies have their volumes altered by changes in temperature and pressure. Thus the volume occupied by a quantity of gas varies inversely as the pressure to which it is subjected, (Boyle's Law); and the volume of gas varies directly as the absolute temperature, (Law of Charles). Since all gases, whether light or heavy, elementary or compound, vary according to these two laws, it follows that the change must be dependent, not on the chemical, but on the physical properties of gaseous substances. Decrease of volume by compression and increase of volume caused by increase of temperature are both due to the overcoming of molecular forces of attraction and repulsion. It follows, then, that if exactly similar quantities of energy cause equal changes in equal volumes of different gases, that equal forces are being overcome; but equal forces exist only among equal numbers of molecules; hence the law enunciated by Avogadro, an Italian chemist, which is as follows: *Equal volumes of gases, whether of the same or of different kinds, contain equal numbers of molecules, under like conditions of temperature and pressure.*

This may be stated in the reverse way:—All molecules occupy equal spaces, when conditions are similar.

4.—Application of this Law.

It is believed that the atoms of elements group themselves into molecules after being set free from combination (see Chapter XIII, page 57). There are reasons, too, for supposing that the molecules of oxygen and hydrogen are each divisible into at least two similar parts (Chapter XL) called atoms, at present. If, then, one writes the molecular equation for the formation of water it stands thus,—$2H_2 + O_2 = 2H_2O$.

Two molecules of hydrogen and one of oxygen form two molecules of water vapor. There is, then, a shrinkage in the number of molecules, consequently in the space occupied by them, consequently in the volume of the resultant gas. Since the number of new molecules is two-thirds that of the mixed gases the volume of the compound should be two-thirds that of the mixed elements, and this agrees with the experimental result.

APPLICATION OF THIS LAW

In general, there will be in the final product of any chemical re-action, when the substances continue as gases throughout the operation, an increase, a diminution, or equality in volume to that which entered into the re-action, according as the atoms re-arrange themselves so as to produce more molecules, fewer molecules, or an equal number of molecules to those which first entered into the re-action. If the number of molecules remain the same at the end as at the beginning, the volume will be the same; if the number of molecules has increased, the volume must have increased in like proportion, and if the number has diminished, the volume must have diminished also in proportion. In all cases the volume is entirely independent of the number of atoms in each molecule, but depends, as already stated, upon the number of molecules.

Some illustrations of this principle may be given, thus —

1. $H_2 + Cl_2 = 2HCl$, no change of volume.
2. $2H_2 + O_2 = 2H_2O$, a contraction of volume from three to two
3. $2H_2O = 2H_2 + O_2$, an increase from two to three.
4. $2N_2O = 2N_2 + O_2$, an increase from two to three.
5. $2NH_3 = N_2 + 3H_2$, an increase to twice the original volume
6. $2CO + O_2 = 2CO_2$, a change from three to two.

CHAPTER XVIII.

Definite Proportions.

EXPERIMENTS.

1. Into a hard glass tube, A, Fig. 14, introduce a weighed quantity of copper oxide, spread in a thin layer. About one gram is a convenient portion to

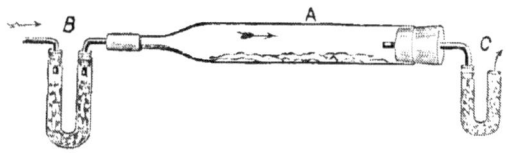

FIG. 14.

work with. Pass a jet of dry hydrogen through this tube, and after all air is expelled heat the tube and contained oxide to redness. Find the weight of the remaining copper. From the result, calculate the weight of oxygen that unites with 63·5 parts by weight of copper.

2. Alter the last experiment by heating the copper that was left in the tube, in a current of air, and find the weight of the black substance (copper oxide) that is formed. Calculate how many parts of oxygen, by weight, unite with 63·5 parts of copper.

3. Vary experiment 1 by passing the hydrogen through a drying tube filled with lumps of caustic potash before it enters the combustion tube, then passing the escaping gas with the results of the combustion through another drying tube, also filled with pieces of caustic potash.

Note.—The student in not to expect an absolutely correct result in quantitative work of this kind. The true result is to be found in the average of many experiments. For this reason a record should be kept of the best results from year to year.

DEFINITE PROPORTIONS. 77

This latter tube must be carefully weighed both before the experiment begins and after it is completed. This will give the weight of the water formed, and from it the weight of hydrogen that unites with 16 parts of oxygen may be found.

4. Heat strongly in a hard glass tube, closed at one end, a weighed quantity of silver nitrate crystals. After all brown fumes cease to come off, find the weight of the resultant solid—pure silver in this case. How many parts, by weight, of NO_3 are in union with 108 of silver?

5. Vary the last experiment by using red oxide of mercury for silver nitrate.

6. Make a solution of caustic potash in a beaker. Stir it well to make it uniform. Put about a couple of grams of hydrochloric acid in a tube, and by means of a burette determine how much of the potash solution is required to just neutralize the acid. Weigh an evaporating dish, put the neutralized solution in it, then evaporate and find the weight of solid residue.

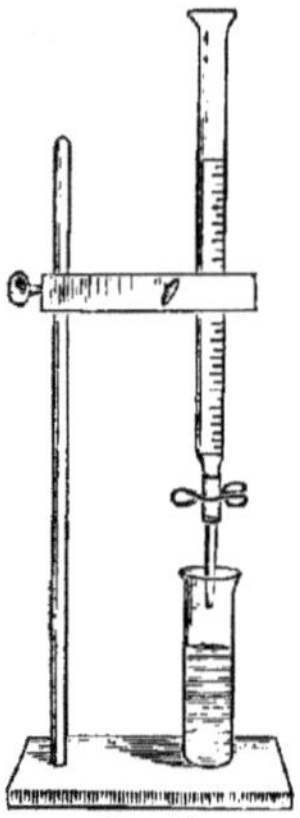

Repeat the experiment with a different quantity of acid to determine if the potash solution and solid residue are proportional to the acid taken.

7. Weigh out about two grams of zinc, and have ready a test-tube nearly filled with dilute sulphuric acid and water, and fitted with a stopper and delivery-tube; drop the zinc into the test-tube and collect the hydrogen given off either in a measuring glass or in a vessel where the volume of the gas can be computed.

FIG 15

Calculate how much hydrogen, by volume, 65 grams of zinc would displace.

Repeat the experiment, using iron and hydrochloric acid.

Find out how much hydrogen 56 grams of iron would displace.

Determine how much hydrogen would be set free by 24 grams of magnesium acting with dilute sulphuric acid.

The result should be approximately 22·4 litres in each case.

The conclusions from such experiments as these show that substances do not take part in chemical actions in random proportions.

This leads to one of the fundamental laws of chemistry, which is, that each element (or radical) unites with other substances in certain fixed and invariable proportions by weight. These proportions are simple multiples of the atomic weight in the case of an element, and of the molecular weight in the case of a compound. See Appendix.

One of the chief differences between a solution and a chemical compound is, that, in the former, varying quantities of the substances may take part in the action; while in the latter, the proportions are perfectly definite. When a centigram of salt is dissolved in a litre of water the result is just as truly a solution as when 10 grams of the salt are used. Another difference is that solutions, unless agitated artificially, are seldom homogeneous, while chemical combination throughout a mass must be absolutely the same in every part.

CHAPTER XIX.

1.—Some Chemical Calculations.

When hydrogen is prepared from zinc and dilute sulphuric acid, the following equation expresses the re-action that takes place:—

$$Zn + H_2SO_4 + H_2O = ZnSO_4 + H_2 + H_2O.$$

From this we see that 65 parts, by weight, of zinc, 98 of sulphuric acid and 18 of water, yield 161 parts, by weight, of zinc sulphate, 2 of hydrogen and 18 of water. The water evidently takes no part in the chemical action, so far as the evolution of hydrogen is concerned, and so may be neglected. The following are examples of some such numerical problems worked out:—

1 Suppose 11·2 grams of hydrogen were required how much zinc and how much sulphuric acid would be used up in obtaining it?

$$Zn + H_2SO_4 + H_2O = ZnSO_4 + H_2 + H_2O.$$

65 "parts" by weight of zinc and 98 of sulphuric acid yield 2 of hydrogen, then 11·2 "parts" by weight of hydrogen come from $65 \times \frac{11\cdot2}{2}$ of zinc and $98 \times \frac{11\cdot2}{2}$ of sulphuric acid, but a *part* may be any unit of weight whatever, since it is a general term, and is used as the unit throughout the problem, hence 11·2 grams of hydrogen come from $65 \times \frac{11\cdot2}{2}$ of zinc and $98 \times \frac{11\cdot2}{2}$ of sulphuric acid.

2. Iron filings treated with hydrochloric acid yield hydrogen according to the equation $Fe + 2HCl = FeCl_2 + H_2$.

If 40 grams of iron were used in the experiment, how much pure hydrochloric acid should be taken, and how much hydrogen would be obtained?

56 parts by weight of iron, and 73 of hydrochloric acid yield 127 of chloride of iron and 2 of hydrogen; then 40 of iron would require $\frac{40}{56}$ of 73 parts of acid and would yield $\frac{40}{56} \times 127$ of the chloride, and $\frac{40}{56} \times 2$ of hydrogen.

3. When oxygen is prepared from chlorate of potassium and manganese dioxide the equation is :—

$KClO_3 + MnO_2 = KCl + MnO_2 + 3O$, hence 122·6 parts by weight of potassic chlorate, heated with 87 parts of manganese dioxide, yield 87 parts of dioxide, 48 of oxygen and 74·6 parts of chloride of potassium. Here also the dioxide is unchanged and may be neglected. Then x grams of the chlorate will yield $\frac{x}{122·6} \times 48$ grams of oxygen, and x grams of oxygen may be obtained from $\frac{x}{48} \times 122·6$ grams of chlorate.

2.—Questions and Exercises.

1. Five grams of sodium are placed on water, and the hydrogen resulting from the chemical action is collected, afterwards the water is evaporated and the white solid that is obtained is weighed. Theoretically, how much hydrogen and how much of this solid would there be?

2. If 5 grams of potassium had been used in the last question what would then have been the answers?

3. If 5 grams of copper oxide, CuO, were reduced in a current of hydrogen, what products would be obtained and how much of each by weight? How much hydrogen by weight would be required to complete this chemical action?

COMBUSTION. 81

4. If 10 grams of lead peroxide, PbO_2, are reduced to lead oxide, PbO, how much oxygen would be given off in the operation, and if this oxygen immediately united with hydrogen, how many grams of the compound would be formed?

5. An excess of iron filings is treated with 50 grams of a solution of hydrochloric acid, containing 25% by weight of pure acid, how many grams of hydrogen will be produced, and how many grams of the compound of iron and acid will be formed?

6. If 50 grams of chlorate of potash were entirely decomposed by heat into potassium chloride and oxygen, and the latter collected over water, then if a jet of burning hydrogen were passed into the jar and kept there until all the oxygen was used up, what would be the weight of the resultant compound?

CHAPTER XX.

1.—Combustion.

It has been customary to classify bodies as combustible or as supporters of combustion. This division, while convenient for use, is not scientifically correct. Combustion is a chemical action in which at least two substances are equally concerned, and the phenomena of combustion are produced by the energy with which the chemical union goes on

Chemical action is usually accompanied by change of temperature, change of volume, or by both these phenomena. When the combination of two substances is accompanied by light and heat (the light as a consequence of the heat) there is said to be either *glowing* or *combustion*—glowing, if a mass of solid matter simply becomes incandescent,—combustion, either if a flame is produced, as in the case of any burning gas, or if the solid, while glowing, alters its chemical composition, usually by oxidation. A red-hot platinum or silver wire glows, so does the fibre of an incandescent lamp; a red-hot magnesium wire burns, so does a splinter of wood.

EXPERIMENTS.

1. In Fig. 16, A is a glass tube about 3 or 4 centimetres in diameter, drawn to about half that diameter at the upper end and closed with a perforated stopper at the lower end; C leads either to an ordinary gas-cock or to a gas-holder. After the air is expelled from A, fire the escaping gas at the top. B is a gas-bag, or gas-holder, filled with oxygen, and the delivery tube D is gradually lowered until the nozzle passes into the interior of A, at the same time the oxygen is being driven out of B by pressure. The gas that escapes through D ought to take fire at the top of A just as the tube D is lowered through the mouth of A, and continue to burn in the interior. Try the experiment using both coal gas and hydrogen passing through C, and oxygen passing through D. Next reverse the operation.

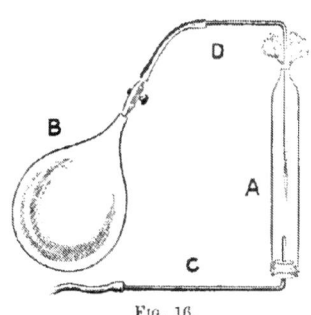

FIG. 16.

(The apparatus of Fig. 34 may be used for this experiment.)

Commonly it is said oxygen does not burn, but supports combustion, while hydrogen burns but does not support combustion. Under what circumstances is this statement correct? Is it ever incorrect?

2. Close the bottom of a lamp chimney with a plate of plaster of Paris by making a paste of the plaster on a sheet of oiled paper and pressing the chimney down in it until the plaster sets. When the plate hardens bore two holes in it, one about a quarter of an inch in diameter near the middle, the other toward one side; cement a piece of glass tubing in the latter and connect it with a gas jet or a supply of hydrogen. Mount the whole in a clamp stand so that the chimney will be upright, and lay flat on top of it a piece of fine wire gauze. Turn on the gas, and when the air is swept out of the chimney light the gas above the gauze. After a minute or so bring a lighted match close below the hole in the plaster plate.

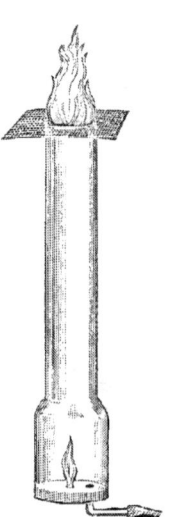

Fig. 17.

What is burning at the top of the chimney, and what is it burning in?

What is burning at the hole and what is it burning in?

3. Fit up an apparatus, as in Fig. 40; put into the flask equal portions of common salt (sodium chloride) and manganese dioxide, then pour on this some sulphuric acid and gently heat the whole. Soon a greenish yellow gas will come off which will collect in the jar at the right. This gas is chlorine. As soon as the jar is full of the gas, as may be seen by the color, drop into it some finely-powdered antimony or arsenic.

4. Prepare another jar of chlorine and lower into it a jet of burning hydrogen.

5. Use the apparatus, Fig. 16, but cause a jet of chlorine to pass through D, and hydrogen through C.

These experiments are sufficient to show that "combustible" and "supporters of combustion" hardly express the relations between the pairs of substances which here enter into combination with each other. A better way to state the case would be, that two kinds of matter which act on each other as do oxygen and hydrogen, or hydrogen and chlorine are *mutually* combustible; or that if there are two gases, A and B, of which A burns in presence of B, it is equally true that B burns in presence of A.

CHAPTER XXI.

1.—Is Air an Element, a Compound, or a Mixture of Gases?

It has been learned that water, one of the substances of most common occurrence, is a compound of two gases. We are now in a position to study another very common substance—the air. The first step will be to determine, if possible, whether it is an element, a compound, or a mixture of two or more gases.

EXPERIMENTS.

1. Cover a cork, about two inches in diameter, with a piece of tin and float on a soup-plate full of water. Take a piece of phosphorus about the size of a pea,

and place it on the cork. Now set fire to the phosphorus, and then cover it quickly with a beaker or small bell jar, placed mouth downwards, as in Fig. 23. Allow it to stand thus for 15 or 20 minutes. After the white fumes have entirely disappeared, lower the plate and jar into water until the water stands at the same height on the inside and the outside of the jar;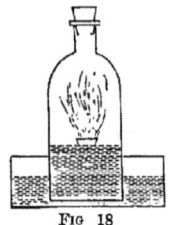

FIG 18

then test the gas by (a) passing a lighted splinter into it, (b) passing a little of it through limewater, (c) driving some of it into a test-tube inverted over mercury, then passing pyrogallate of potash into this tube. In the last case, observe if a material darkening of the liquid takes place after it enters the tube, or if there is any considerable decrease in the volume of the gas.

Why did the water rise in the jar?

What were the white fumes composed of?

How does the remaining gas differ from air?

What was taken from the air by the phosphorus?

Is the remaining gas hydrogen?

2. Invert a test-tube of air over mercury, pass into it some pyrogallate of potash and let it stand.

EXPLANATION.

Pyrogallate of potash absorbs free oxygen and becomes brown colored. Oxygen in combination is not thus taken up.

3 Wet the inside of a bell jar with water, and drop into it some fine iron filings. Then shake the jar so that the inside may become closely sprinkled with the filings.

Place the jar, mouth downward, over a soup-plate filled with water, and allow the whole to stand for a day or two. Carefully invert the jar by slipping the hand under its mouth, and as it is turned mouth upward, allow the water in it to run to the bottom; thus an influx of air is prevented. Test the gas in the jar with a burning splinter.

What became of the iron?

What is the composition of the red substance?

2.—Questions.

1. Pyrogallate of potash turns brown in the atmosphere and takes part of it up. What is the inference?

2. Is air a mixture of at least two substances, a chemical compound of two substances, or a single element? What reasons for the answer?

EXPLANATION.

The gas that was left in the jar after the phosphorus burned, and the fumes were absorbed, was almost entirely **nitrogen.**

3.—Volumetric Composition of the Atmosphere.

The quantities, by volume, in which oxygen and nitrogen are mixed in the atmosphere may be determined by causing the oxygen to unite with some substance to form an oxide which is soluble, or which condenses to solid or liquid condition and whose volume may be neglected.

EXPERIMENT.

Experiment 1, page 84, may be used to find approximately the quantity of oxygen in air by measuring the volume of the jar and measuring the water that rises into it, but bubbles of gas are likely to escape at the beginning of the experiment so that the full quantity of air is not present to be acted on.

Try the experiment and calculate the percentage of oxygen present. Why does gas escape?

A glass tube about 20 inches long is closed air-tight at one end, a piece of freshly-cut phosphorus is passed up to this end, supported by a thin wire, if necessary, and the open end of the tube is immersed in water. After twenty-four hours bring the water to the same level inside and outside the tube. Compare the volume of gas now in the tube with that originally there by measuring heights.

Vary this experiment as follows: measure the contents of a flask,

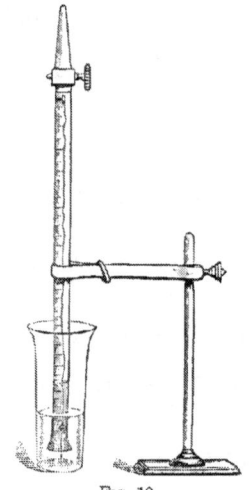

FIG. 19.

about one litre capacity, prepare a chalk cup in a base, as in experiment 7, page 44, put a piece of phosphorus in it, invert the flask over it and, after all chemical action has ceased, measure the water that rises in the neck of the flask.

3. Pass into a eudiometer 20 or 30 cc. of dry air and about half as much hydrogen; after the gases mix explode them. Since two volumes of hydrogen unite with one of oxygen and the water vapor condenses to liquid, whose volume need not be considered, one-third of the decrease in the volume of mixed gases is due to

the oxygen that was in the air and that combined with the hydrogen.

EXPLANATION.

The average of a number of such experiments shows that air is about 21% oxygen and 79% nitrogen, by volume.

By weight, the percentage is somewhat different, as the following calculation shows:—

21 volumes of oxygen are equivalent in weight to $21 \times 16 = 336$ volumes of hydrogen.

79 volumes of nitrogen are equal in weight to $79 \times 14 = 1106$ volumes of hydrogen. 100 parts by volume of air when expressed in terms of the weight of one part of hydrogen = 1442, of which 336 are represented by oxygen and 1106 by nitrogen.

$\frac{336}{1442} = 23.3\%$ oxygen and $\frac{1106}{1442} = 76.7\%$ nitrogen.

Besides the two gases mentioned, ordinary air contains some water vapor, a little carbon dioxide, and minute quantities of the rare gases argon, helium, krypton, neon, and xenon. For common purposes, however, air may be considered as a mixture of oxygen and hydrogen in the proportions given.

The reasons for believing that air is a mixture, not a chemical compound, are chiefly the following:—

> (1) Pyrogallate of potash will separate oxygen from nitrogen of the air, but pyrogallate of potash absorbs only free oxygen, not that which is in combination.

(2) A mixture of oxygen and nitrogen may be made which cannot be distinguished from air, either chemically or physically, yet there is neither change of temperature nor of volume, one or both of which are the common phenomena of chemical action.

(3) The gases are not present in the proportions corresponding to their atomic weights, or in simple multiples of their atomic weights, yet they could not be present in other proportions if air were a compound.

(4) Air is soluble in water, and if the dissolved air be expelled by heating or by the air pump, and the gases collected, the oxygen and nitrogen are found not in the same proportion in which they were before solution; the expelled gases contain about 35% of oxygen. If air were a compound the proportions could not vary even in solution. The relatively high solubility of oxygen is a factor in the support of gill-breathing animals.

(5) Air that has been collected at different places gives, on analysis, slightly different proportions by weight.

(6) When air is liquefied, and the temperature slowly raised, the nitrogen volatilizes first and leaves oxygen behind. If it were a compound the substance as a whole would change to vapor, as water does, not one constituent of it only.

CHAPTER XXII.

1.—Nitrogen—Its Properties and Preparation.

EXPERIMENTS.

1. The simplest method of obtaining nitrogen is by burning phosphorus or some other combustible substance, which will form a solid oxide or a readily soluble one, in a bell jar over water. The experiments of the last chapter illustrate this preparation.

2. Nitrogen may also be obtained by heating **ammonium nitrite** which breaks up as follows:—

$$NH_4NO_2 = 2H_2O + 2N.$$

3. Prepare a hydrogen apparatus with a delivery tube as shown in Fig. 20. After the hydrogen is burning freely at the mouth of the tube invert a gas cylinder over it so that the mouth of the cylinder will be under water in the dish. Watch closely what occurs. The instant the flame goes out disconnect the delivery tube from the flask. After the water has ceased to rise in the cylinder slip a glass cover under it and turn it mouth upwards, but do not let the water run out, else air will become mixed with the gas in the cylinder. Test this gas as in the previous experiment.

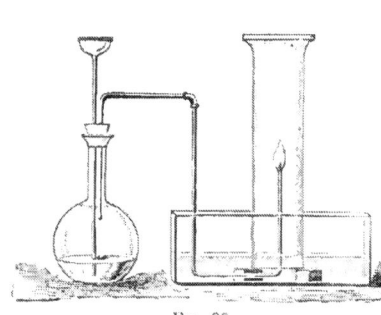

FIG. 20.

Tabulate the properties and appearance of nitrogen oxygen, hydrogen and air.

4. The apparatus represented in Fig. 21 may be used for preparing nitrogen by passing air over red-hot copper. A is a U-tube filled with calcic chloride, B is a straight tube filled with fine, bright copper filings, and C is a large-mouthed bottle used as a gas-holder, one of its tubes passing through the cork, the other passing to the bottom of the bottle; D is a piece of rubber-tubing attached to the latter of these tubes in order to convert it into a syphon, and draw off the water from the bottle. E is a spring clip which may be kept slightly open by putting a small wedge in it. On starting the experiment, the bottle must be full of water. When the copper has been made red-hot, the syphon must be made to act *very slowly* by regulating the clip, and as the water flows out of the bottle, air is drawn through the U-tube and passes over the red-hot copper. The nitrogen is collected in the bottle.

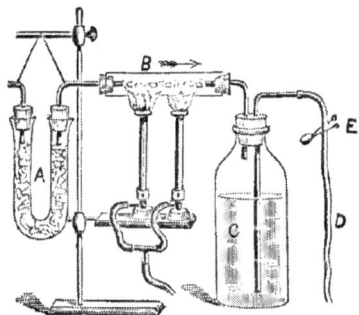

Fig. 21.

2.—Notes on Nitrogen.

Nitrogen: symbol, N.; atomic weight, 14; molecular weight, 28; molecular volume, 2.

On account of its chemical inertness the compounds of nitrogen are often unstable and are frequently liable to sudden and violent decomposition; for example, nitro-glycerine, chloride of nitrogen, picric acid, and nitro powders.

Nitrogen occurs free in the air, of which it forms by volume 79%, and by weight 77%; it is also a constituent of almost all organic substances, and enters into the composition of a large number of inorganic compounds.

3.—Uses of Nitrogen.

Nitrogen serves to dilute the oxygen of the air, so that it may be suitable for the support of animal life. It is essential for vegetable growth, though probably not used to any considerable extent in the form of pure gas. The value of animal manures is chiefly on account of their nitrogenous ingredients which are leached out in the soil and absorbed by the roots of the plants. The nitrogen of the air is *fixed* in the upper layers of soil in the form of compounds, chiefly nitrates and nitrites through the agency bacteria. These compounds are then available for plant absorption.

CHAPTER XXIII.

Compounds of Nitrogen and Oxygen.

Nitrogen and oxygen do not unite directly to form compounds as do hydrogen and oxygen; there are, however, five oxides of nitrogen known, all of them being obtained by the decomposition of other compounds.

These are :—

Nitrous oxide or nitrogen monoxide	N_2O,
Nitric " " dioxide	NO,
Nitrogen trioxide	N_2O_3,
Nitrogen peroxide or nitrogen tetroxide	NO_2, or N_2O_4,
Nitrogen pentoxide	N_2O_5.

1.—Nitrous Oxide.

EXPERIMENTS.

1. Put 25 grams of commercial ammonium nitrate, NH_4NO_3, into an oxygen generating apparatus, connected with three bottles, as in Fig. 22. The first bottle should contain a solution of ferrous sulphate, the second

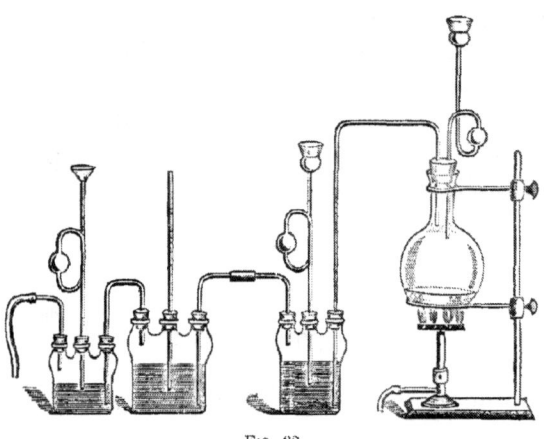

FIG. 22.

a solution of caustic potash, and the third, water. Heat the nitrate gently, and nitrogen monoxide will be given off. Thus prepared, the gas will be found mixed with nitrogen dioxide and chlorine gas. The first will be removed by passing through the ferrous sulphate solution, and the second by passing through the caustic potash solution.

If the nitrate be chemically pure, the wash bottles may be omitted. The re-action may be thus represented:

$$NH_4NO_3 = 2H_2O + N_2O.$$

2. Collect several jars of the gas over warm water and perform the following experiments:—

(*a*) Plunge a lighted taper into the first jar; also test it with a glowing splinter, as in the case of oxygen.

(*b*) Burn a piece of phosphorus, carbon or sulphur in another of the jars.

(*c*) Explode a mixture of the gas with hydrogen.

(*d*) Place another jar, mouth downward, over *cold* water, and let it stand for 24 hours. Vary this experiment by filling a test-tube with the gas, put a little water in it, close the mouth tightly by putting the thumb over it, then shake the water up with the gas, invert the tube, dip the mouth under water and remove the thumb. Test the water that rose in the tube with litmus.

3. Try the effect of dry nitrous oxide upon litmus.

4. How could nitrous oxide be distinguished from oxygen?

5. Using the apparatus of Fig. 20, burn a jet of hydrogen in nitrous oxide. What are the substances formed? Write equation. What change in volume, if any, takes place during the combustion? Explain.

6. Try if a mixture of hydrogen and nitrous oxide will explode when an electric spark is passed through it.

2.—Notes on Nitrous Oxide.

Nitrous Oxide: formula, N_2O, molecular weight, 44; vapor density, 22.

"Laughing gas" is an old name for this compound, derived from the effects it produces when inhaled. It will also produce temporary unconsciousness to pain, and is, therefore, used as an anæsthetic, especially in dentistry.

Nitrous oxide is largely soluble in cold water and supports combustion freely, because it readily decomposes into nitrogen and oxygen. The heat of a glowing match is sufficient for this purpose.

3.—Nitric Oxide or Nitrogen Dioxide.

EXPERIMENTS

1. Place some copper clippings in a hydrogen generating apparatus similar to that in Fig. 5, add some warm water, and then pour down the funnel tube some strong nitric acid. The gas that first forms should be allowed to escape. The re-action may be thus represented:—

$$3Cu + 8HNO_3 = 3Cu(NO_3)_2 + 4H_2O + 2NO.$$

This re-action is really the result of two separate and successive ones, thus —

(1). $Cu + 2HNO_3 = Cu(NO_3)_2 + 2H.$

(2). $3H + HNO_3 = NO + 2H_2O.$

The explanation of this will be found in chap. XXIV, sect. 3.

2. Place a tube full of gas, mouth downwards, over a small quantity of water in a dish, then pass air, a little

at a time, into the tube.* Test the water with litmus both before the air is passed in, then again after the brown fumes have disappeared.

Unless the operator is careful in this experiment a wrong result will be obtained. When the tube is filled with the gas it should be removed to a clean plate with a little water on it, so that the gas will be tested and not a solution of the brown fumes formed by bubbles of it coming in contact with air.

3. Test the gas with a glowing splinter, a blazing splinter, a burning taper, a piece of slightly-ignited phosphorus, a piece of brightly-burning phosphorus.

4. Lift a test-tube full of the gas and place it, mouth downwards, in a vessel containing a cold solution of copperas (ferrous sulphate), $FeSO_4$.

Vary this experiment as follows:—

Pour some well-cooled solution of ferrous sulphate, $FeSO_4$, into a bottle full of the gas; then hold the hand over the bottle's mouth and shake vigorously.

4.—Questions and Exercises.

Is the colorless gas soluble to any considerable extent?

Is the colored gas soluble?

Is it an acid forming substance?

Does N_2O oxidize to NO by heating in air?

Nitric oxide forms a test for free oxygen. Explain why it is a test?

Nitric oxide is a convenient agent for the separation of oxygen from nitrogen in air. Explain fully how it may be used for this purpose.

Nitric oxide contains relatively twice as much oxygen as nitrous oxide does, yet a blazing splinter or candle instantly goes out in it. What is the reason?

---

* The air may readily be driven into the tube by using an empty flask fitted up like the one in fig. . When water is poured down the funnel, air is forced out through the delivery tube.

5. Pass oxygen into a jar of nitric oxide over water very slowly so that the brown fumes may disappear as rapidly as formed. Account for the result obtained.

What evidence is there that when nitric acid acts on copper more than one oxide of nitrogen is formed?

Try to determine if these gases are produced to the same extent when cold acid, diluted one half with water, is used as when hot concentrated acid is employed.

5.—Notes on Nitric Oxide.

Nitric oxide: formula, NO; molecular weight, 30; vapor density, 15.

Nitric oxide condenses to a liquid at—11°C. and a pressure of 104 atmospheres. It does not unite with water to form an acid. One test for this gas is its re-action with air or free oxygen; another is that with a solution of ferrous sulphate a dark ring or layer is formed on the liquid, as seen in experiment 4. This gas changes by mere contact with free oxygen into a higher oxide of nitrogen. This oxidation results in the formation of NO_2, the brown, soluble, acid forming gas.

6.—Composition by Volume of Nitrous Oxide and Nitric Oxide.

Prepare a hard glass tube, bent as A in the Fig. 23. Fill this with washed nitrous oxide gas, having previously dropped into the tube a piece of sodium, or of potassium, about as large as a pea. Dip the mouth of the tube, when filled with gas, under mercury, and by jarring it, get the sodium into a position just below A. Then

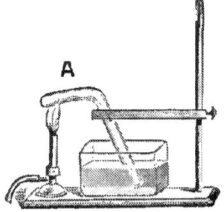

FIG. 23.

heat it strongly. The hot sodium decomposes the nitrous oxide to form oxide of sodium and the nitrogen is left. The volume of the nitrogen should be the same as that of the original gas.

Nitric oxide may be decomposed in the same way, but the volume of nitrogen in this case is only one half that of the oxide taken.

Nitrous oxide, then, contains its own volume of nitrogen; that is, when decomposed each molecule yields one molecule of nitrogen, N_2. The molecular weight of nitrous oxide is 44, and since the nitrogen atoms account for 28 of these units the oxygen must have supplied the other 16, hence the formula of the gas is N_2O.

In the case of nitric oxide there is half the volume of nitrogen remaining, hence each molecule of the gas contained half a molecule, or one atom of nitrogen; and since the molecular weight is 30 the formula must be NO.

This compound of nitrogen is commercially important because of its employment in the preparation of sulphuric acid, see Chap. XXXVII.

7.—Nitrogen Trioxide.

EXPERIMENT.

Fit a flask with a cork and delivery tube, and place on a retort stand, as in Fig. 24. To the delivery tube attach a U-tube, immersed in a freezing mixture of salt and snow. Connect the other end of the U-tube with a glass tube leading to a vessel containing ice-water. Place 10 grams of starch in the flask and cover with nitric acid. Gently heat the generating flask and nitrogen trioxide will be plentifully produced, part of it being condensed in the U-tube, and the remainder passing on into the ice-water.

Instead of starch, white arsenic, As_2O_3, may be used.

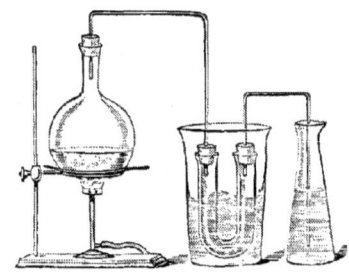

Fig. 24.

The re-action in this case may be thus represented:—

$$2HNO_3 + As_2O_3 + 2H_2O = N_2O_3 + 2H_3AsO_4 \text{ (Arsenic acid)}.$$

Notice the color of the gas. It is condensed to a liquid by a temperature of $-18°C$. Try to collect some of the gas over water. Has it any smell?

The gas, as condensed in the U-tube, is green in color. This is owing to nitrogen peroxide being mixed with it. If the generating flask be disconnected and a current of nitric oxide passed through the U-tube, the brown gas that passes off, if again condensed, will be indigo blue in color; this will be pure nitrogen trioxide.

By using for a condenser a piece of thick glass tubing drawn out, as shown in Fig. 25, the liquid may be preserved; for by using a blowpipe flame the tube may readily be sealed at A and B; and internal pressure will then prevent the fluid from evaporating. The tube must be strong enough, however, to withstand the pressure.

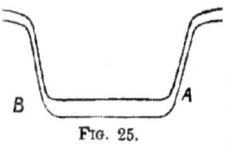

Fig. 25.

Nitrogen trioxide is known only in the liquid condition, when it is removed from the cooling fluid it decomposes into substances, one of which is NO_2. The trioxide, however, with alkaline solutions forms salts that are fairly stable, and that contain the acid radical NO_2, hence are **nitrites.**

8.—Nitrogen Tetroxide or Nitrogen Peroxide.

This gas is prepared by heating lead nitrate and condensing the gas, as in the case of the trioxide. It is the substance most largely formed when nitric oxide comes in contact with air. This substance has the formula NO_2, and in union with cold water forms a mixture of nitrous and nitric acids, thus, $2NO_2 + H_2O = HNO_3 + HNO_2$. It is a valuable oxidizing agent, on account of the ease with which it undergoes decomposition into nitric oxide and oxygen. The manufacture of sulphuric acid illustrates one application of this.

9.—Nitrogen Pentoxide.

There is still another oxide of nitrogen, viz., the pentoxide, N_2O_5, but it is difficult of preparation and derives its chief importance from forming nitric acid with water. When freed it breaks up into NO_2 and oxygen.

10.—Law of Multiple Proportions.

These oxides of nitrogen illustrate the law of **Multiple Proportions** in chemistry. Beginning with the lowest oxide and going to the highest, there are successively one, two, three, four and five volumes of oxygen united with two volumes of nitrogen. Expressed in another way, the quantity of oxygen, which is the variable element here, is an integral multiple in every case, both of unit volume and of atomic weight. The relative quantities of oxygen are in the ratio of the numbers 1, 2, 3, 4 and 5, and these are the only proportions in which the elements can be made to unite.

The law may be stated as follows :—If two substances form more than one compound, the proportions in which they enter into combination are simple multiples of their atomic weights.

If the substances are gases, the statement applies to unit volumes as well as to weights   See appendix.

CHAPTER XXIV.

1.—Acids of Nitrogen.

The most important of the acids of nitrogen is HNO_3, **nitric acid**, formed by the union of nitrogen pentoxide and water. There are two others, though, known by the salts they form with alkaline bases, viz., **hyponitrous**, HNO, produced by the union of nitrous oxide and water; thus, $N_2O + H_2O = 2HNO$; and **nitrous**, HNO_2, formed by solution of nitrogen trioxide; thus, $N_2O_3 + H_2O = 2HNO_2$. The nitrites are found in decomposing organic substances, so that their presence in water is an indication of impurity. A simple test for them is to try if the suspected matter will decolorize a faintly purple solution of permanganate of potassium. This salt readily parts with oxygen and becomes colorless, nitrites take up oxygen to form nitrates, hence the deoxidation of the permanganate, $KMnO_4$, shows the presence, probably, of nitrites.

DEFINITION.

An oxide which unites chemically with water, and thus forms an acid, is called an **anhydride**, thus,

$$N_2O_5, \quad N_2O_3, \quad CO_2, \quad SO_3,$$

are respectively nitric, nitrous, carbonic, and sulphuric anhydrides.

2.—Nitric Acid—Preparation and Properties.

EXPERIMENTS.

1. Put into a tubulated glass retort 30 grams of powdered nitrate of potash, KNO_3, and an equal weight of strong sulphuric acid, H_2SO_4. Place the end of the retort in a flask, which is made to float on a basin of water, as in Fig. 26. Apply heat to the retort. Soon a yellowish colored liquid distils over and is collected in the cool flask. The re-action may be represented as taking place in two successive stages, the first requiring a comparatively low, the second a high, temperature.

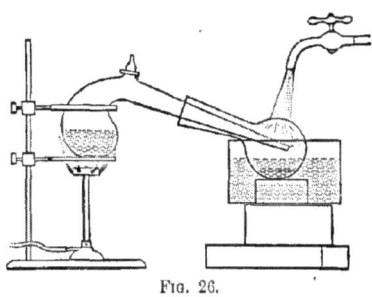

FIG. 26.

(*a*) $2KNO_3 + H_2SO_4 = HKSO_4 + HNO_3 + KNO_3$.

On increasing the heat more acid comes off, the second re-action being represented as follows:—

(*b*) $HKSO_4 + KNO_3 = K_2SO_4 + HNO_3$.

Sodium nitrate, $NaNO_3$, may be used instead of potassium nitrate in the preparation of nitric acid; in fact the former is generally employed when the acid is to be manufactured on a large scale.

2. Heat a few drops of the acid until nearly boiling, then hold close to its surface a piece of glowing charcoal. Vary this by heating strongly some fine charcoal dust, then dropping on it some strong nitric acid.

What chemical action goes on?

Upon what evidence is the answer based?

What passes off at same time?

Is there any evidence that nitric acid acts as an oxidizing agent?

3 Warm a few drops of the acid in a small evaporating dish, then, keeping at some distance, drop into it a bit of phosphorus.

4. Put strong nitric acid, to a depth of half-an-inch, into a test-tube, and plug the mouth of the tube loosely with some paper saturated with turpentine, then heat the acid to boiling.

What does the brown gas passing off from the acid indicate?

Turpentine has the composition $C_{10}H_{16}$; show the relation of these constituents to the chemical result.

Repeat the experiment, but use instead of the saturated paper a plug of wool or woollen cloth.

Try if benzine, C_6H_6; alcohol, C_2H_6O; or coal oil, a mixture of hydrocarbons, may be used instead of turpentine.

What conclusion from these observations as to the properties of the acid?

5. Immerse some undyed wool, silk, a piece of quill, or other white, animal substance in a little of the acid.

6. Add a few drops of the acid to a solution of indigo.

7. Place some copper filings in the bottom of a test-tube, and then pour in some of the acid. When all action has ceased, evaporate to dryness the solution which has been formed.

In this experiment one would naturally expect hydrogen to come off; notice, however, that the escaping gas is brown in color, does not burn, and is soluble. Evidently, therefore, an oxide of nitrogen is given off.

Repeat the experiment with other metals. Try if the results are the same when zinc is put in cold, dilute nitric acid and in hot concentrated acid.

3.—Notes on Nitric Acid.

The two most important chemical properties of nitric acid are its power of oxidation, and its decomposition by nascent hydrogen. The former is illustrated by its action with charcoal, sulphur, phosphorus, yellow oxide of lead and the *ous* salts of many metals. When the acid is heated it breaks down into oxide of hydrogen, an oxide of nitrogen and free oxygen, generally thus,— $2HNO_3 = H_2O + 2NO_2 + O$. The NO_2 liberated in this way is also a strong oxidizing agent, becoming reduced to NO.

The general effect of nascent hydrogen on nitric acid is to bring about a decomposition, though the products of breaking down are quite variable, depending on conditions of temperature, concentration, and available hydrogen. (See Remsen, page 279.) They are all due, however, to the deoxidation of the acid by the hydrogen.

$$2HNO_3 + 2H = 2H_2O + 2NO_2,$$
$$2HNO_3 + 6H = 4H_2O + 2NO,$$

are two typical re-actions.

The acid undergoes partial decomposition, as shown by the brown fumes, when raised to its boiling point, hence, in its preparation, heat enough only is employed to cause the first stage of chemical action between the nitrate and the sulphuric acid.

4.—Tests.

1. Nitric acid heated with copper filings in air gives off brown fumes of NO_2.

2. Add two or three drops of sulphuric acid to a little of the solution supposed to contain nitric acid, put the mixture in an evaporating dish or tube and cool it, then pour cautiously down the side of the vessel some clear ferrous sulphate solution A brown discoloration shows the presence of nitric acid. This test answers equally well for nitrates. If circumstances permit, a small crystal of ferrous sulphate may be dropped into the mixture, and the brown layer will appear as the crystal dissolves. The brown substance is a combination of the sulphate and nitric oxide $(FeSO_4)NO$.

3. Nitric acid oxidizes and bleaches indigo solution.

5 —Nitrates.

EXPERIMENTS.

1. Heat some potassium nitrate until it melts, then drop into it some charcoal. What decomposition must have taken place in the salt?

Does ammonium nitrate give a similar result?

2. Make a mixture of finely-powdered charcoal, sulphur and potassium nitrate, heat a *little* of this on mica.

What does the rate of burning indicate?

6.—Notes on Nitrates.

Nitrates are soluble, and yield oxygen when heated, thus,—$KNO_3 = KNO_2 + O$.

To this ammonium nitrate, NH_4NO_3, seems to be an exception, probably because it undergoes a deoxidation similar to that of nitric acid in presence of nascent hydrogen. When gently heated it yields, as we have seen, $N_2O + 2H_2O$; but when strongly heated breaks up into water, oxygen and free nitrogen, the oxygen being first given off thus :—

$$NH_4NO_3 = NH_4NO_2 + O = 2N + 2H_2O + O.$$

The nitrates of most metallic bases, when heated form the oxide of the metal, free oxygen and nitrogen peroxide, thus :—

$$Pb(NO_3)_2 = PbO + 2NO_2 + O.$$

Those of the alkaline bases potassium and sodium lose oxygen on heating, become first reduced to nitrites and finally to the oxides of the metals.

OCCURRENCE OF NITRATES.

These are formed in soil in which there are basic materials and in which organic substances are decaying. Very large natural deposits of nitrates of sodium and potassium exist in the nearly rainless regions of northern Chili. This material is exported to Europe in great quantities for use in alkali manufactures.

7 —Uses of Nitric Acid and Nitrates.

Compounds of nitrogen, generally nitrates or their derivatives, are largely employed in the manufacture of explosives. For instance, gunpowder is a mixture of sulphur, charcoal and potassium nitrate, nitro-glycerine, picric acid, and nitro powders are other illustrations.

Nitrates are valuable as fertilizers, because they are a source of nitrogen, a necessary substance for plant growth. Certain bacteria, existing plentifully in soils, fix the nitrogen of the air in the form of nitrates and these being soluble are taken up through the roots of the plants.

Chemically, nitric acid and nitrates are used as oxidizing agents

---

CHAPTER XXV.

1.—Nitrogen and Hydrogen.

There is one well-known combination of nitrogen and hydrogen—ammonia, which is of very common occurrence in compounds, and is of considerable economic importance on account of its use in the arts.

EXPERIMENTS.

1. Take about 20 grams of dry ammonic chloride and an equal quantity of dry quicklime; powder them finely in a mortar. Then transfer the mixture to a flask with tightly-fitting cork and long tube bent upwards. Heat gently. Hold a large test-tube over the delivery tube, and fill it with gas by downward displacement of air as in Fig. 26.

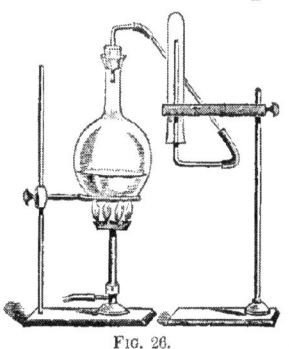
Fig. 26.

$$2NH_4Cl + CaO = CaCl_2 + 2NH_3 + H_2O.$$

What evidence is there that a gas has come off from the mixture?

How may its presence be known?

2. Pass some of the gas into reddened litmus. Upon the result of this, devise a means of knowing when a bottle is full of this gas.

3. Pour 4 or 5 drops of hydrochloric acid into a large beaker that has been warmed, and, by shaking, spread the acid over the bottom and sides of the vessel, then hold it mouth downwards over the delivery tube.

Why is the result in this case different from that in experiment 1?

What is the white cloud in the beaker?

From experiment 2, what result might be expected when ammonia is brought into contact with an acid?

Are the white clouds made up of a mixture of ammonia and acid vapor, or of a combination of them? Why?

A more convenient method of obtaining ammonia gas is by heating the spirits of hartshorn, the *liquor ammoniæ* of the drug shops. Hartshorn is only a solution of ammonia gas in water.

4. Fit a flask with a rubber stopper and tube, as in Fig. 27. Place in the flask a little hartshorn and heat it to boiling When ammonia gas begins to escape from the tube, invert it, and place the open end in some water colored pink with litmus.

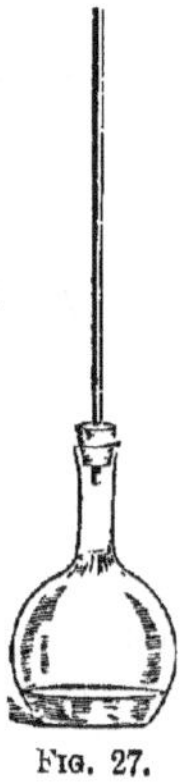

5. Fill a graduated tube, such as a eudiometer, with dried ammonia gas over mercury, then lift the tube and place it mouth downward in cold water To what extent is the gas soluble?

6. Fill a large test-tube with ammonia gas over mercury. Take a piece of porous charcoal (that from pine wood, or pine bark is best), hold it in a flame until it begins to burn over most of its surface, then pass it into the tube without raising the latter out of the mercury; let the whole stand for a couple of hours. Is the result due to any action of the mercury?

Fig. 27.

Will hot charcoal absorb air in a similar way?

Place the charcoal in a test-tube fitted with a stopper and delivery tube, the latter passing into an inverted test-tube. Heat the charcoal for some time, then test the gas in the inverted tube for solubility

Does the charcoal give up the ammonia again.

Where did the gas disappear to?

7. Fit up apparatus, as in Fig. 28. The tube A is a large test-tube drawn out to a nozzle about ⅜ of an inch

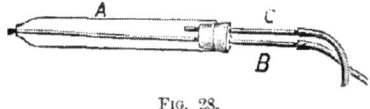

Fig. 28.

in diameter, the tube, B, must slide somewhat freely through the perforation in the stopper and just project beyond the opening in A ; C is connected with an oxygen supply, and B is joined to the flask in which ammonia is generated. When the current of ammonia is passing through B try to light it, then turn on the oxygen and after it is escaping from the nozzle try again to ignite the ammonia.

Vary the experiment again by pulling B backwards until it projects through the cork only as far as C does ; as the mixed gases escape from the nozzle try to ignite them.

Will ammonia burn in air?

Will it burn in oxygen?

Will a mixture of ammonia and oxygen burn?

How is the power of oxygen to support combustion affected by concentration?

Let some oxygen bubble through a strong warm solution of ammonia in a flask, then try if the escaping gas will burn.

EXPLANATION.

When ammonia burns with oxygen it is decomposed, thus :—

$$2NH_3 + 3O = 2N + 3H_2O.$$

8. Form about a foot of platinum wire into a spiral by winding it around a lead pencil or bit of glass rod. Heat some hartshorn in a flask until ammonia is coming off, then heat the wire red hot and suspend it in the escaping

gas. If kept in the neck of the flask just where the ammonia and air are mixed the spiral should glow for several minutes, while in the air it almost instantly cools.

The explanation is that the red-hot platinum promotes the union of the ammonia and the oxygen of the air, the resultant products being those of the combustion of ammonia, and the heat developed in the chemical action is sufficient to keep the platinum at the glowing point.

When ammonia is burned in oxygen why does not an oxide of nitrogen form as well as that of hydrogen?

2.—Ammonium and its Compounds.

The name *ammonium* has been given to a substance having the formula NH_4 which forms a group of compounds similar to those of potassium; for example:—

$KCl, NH_4Cl; KNO_3, NH_4NO_3; KOH, NH_4OH;$
$KC_2H_3O_2, NH_4C_2H_3O_2; K_2CO_3, (NH_4)_2CO_3$, etc.

Ammonium has never been obtained in an uncombined state, for, when set free, it at once becomes decomposed into ammonia and hydrogen.

The following experiment is sometimes given as a demonstration of the existence of this metallic radical. The result is interesting, at least.

EXPERIMENT.

Drop some pieces of sodium amalgam* into a strong solution of ammonium chloride. When the mass swells up feel it with the fingers. What gas is escaping?

---
*Mercury forms with several metals, combinations that are analogous to solutions, though they are frequently solid. These are the amalgams. They are not chemical compounds, for the elements composing them may be quite variable in quantity. Mercury forms amalgams only with some of the metals, never with non-metals. Sodium amalgam is prepared as in ex 3, page 27. If enough sodium has been used the amalgam will be a brittle, silvery-grey solid. It must be kept in a tightly-stoppered bottle.

Does ammonia come off from the chloride solution?

What remains of the amalgam?

Taste a drop of the liquid. Does it resemble the original chloride solution?

Common salt is sodium chloride. Is there any evidence of union of the sodium and chlorine?

EXPLANATION.

It is thought that the swollen, soapy feeling mass that forms in the ammonium chloride is ammonium amalgam that decomposes into mercury, hydrogen and ammonia. The entire re-action being:—

(1) Mercury and sodium form sodium amalgam.
(2) Sodium amalgam and ammonium chloride yield ammonium amalgam and sodium chloride.
(3) Ammonium amalgam breaks up into ammonia, mercury and hydrogen.

The metallic ammonium would thus be a hydride of ammonia.

3.—Ammonium Hydroxide.

When potassium is thrown on water, the water molecules are broken up into hydroxyl radicals and hydrogen, the former uniting with the potassium to form potassic hydrate, and the latter escaping as free gas. Similarly ammonia with water forms a hydroxide, but the atom of hydrogen instead of going free changes ammonia into ammonium which combines with the hydroxyl, forming NH_4OH, thus:—$NH_3 + H_2O = NH_4OH$

Hydroxides of metals are basic and with acids form salts of the metals and water, thus:—

$$KOH + HNO_3 = KNO_3 + H_2O$$
$$2NH_4OH + H_2SO_4 = (NH_4)_2SO_4 + 2H_2O$$

4.—Detection of Ammonia.

It is of importance that ammonia should be capable of easy and accurate detection, as its presence in water to any appreciable extent is usually an indication of the unfitness of that water for drinking. The following form the tests generally applied.—

1. Pungent smell, if present in quantity.

2. Dissolve any ammonium salt in water, pour into this solution, in a test-tube, some solution of an alkaline hydroxide, then heat, and the odor of ammonia should be perceived.

3. When present in minute quantities, as it frequently is in drinking water, ammonia is best detected by what is known as Nessler's test: "To a solution of potassic iodide add solution of mercuric chloride until the precipitate formed just ceases to be re-dissolved, then add an equal volume of strong solution of caustic potash, and allow the whole to stand until clear. A few drops of this solution will give a yellowish-red precipitate, with a very slight trace of ammonia."

Notes on Ammonia.

Ammonia: symbol, NH_3; mol. vol., 2; vapor density, 8.5.

Ammonium is a *strongly alkaline, monad base.*

Ammonia is very soluble in cold water; it becomes a liquid at—40°C; and may even be frozen at—75°C.

5.—Sources.

Ammonia occurs in animal excretions and in decomposing animal substances, which always contain nitrogen in some combination. The source of commercial ammonia is as a bye-product in the preparation of illuminating gas.

Bituminous coal contains a little nitrogen, and in the distillation this passes off in union with some of the hydrogen as ammonia, which is dissolved in the water in which the volatile substances are washed. This solution is treated for the separation of the ammonia as salts of ammonium, chiefly the chloride and sulphate.

6.—Preparation.

Any of the ammonium salts heated with one of the non-volatile alkaline oxides or hydroxides will yield ammonia gas, because the alkali of the oxide displaces ammonium from the salt, thus :—

$$2NH_4Cl + Ca(HO)_2 = CaCl_2 + 2H_2O + 2NH_3.$$

7.—Uses.

Ammonia is valuable as a fertilizer for plant growth on account of the nitrogen in its composition. Barnyard manures, for instance, contain ammonia, and this is one important source of their value for enriching soil.

Ammonia is also used as a cleansing agent, and in some manufacturing operations such as dyeing. Its most important application, however, is to refrigerating processes. Its great solubility and its rapid volatilization from solution, or condensed liquid, either at raised temperature or reduced pressure, make it a most effective and convenient substance to employ in cooling operations. It has thus come into wide use in refrigerating plants for factories, ships, storehouses, hotels, etc., and for the manufacture of artificial ice, even in tropical countries.

8.—Questions and Exercises.

1. Complete the following equations —

$$NH_4HO + HNO_3 =$$
$$2NH_4HO + H_2SO_4 =$$
$$NH_4NO_2 + KHO =$$
$$2NH_4OH + H_2CO_3 =$$
$$NH_4Cl + NaOH =$$

2. Potassium chloride and potassium nitrate are written KCl and KNO_3 respectively, while ammonia has the formula NH_3, but the chloride and nitrate are written NH_4Cl and NH_4NO_3. How is the extra atom of hydrogen accounted for?

3. Ammonium nitrate has its formula written NH_4NO_3, what objection is there to writing it $N_2H_4O_3$?

4. What weight of ammonia gas can be obtained from 214 grams of ammonic chloride?

5. What weight of quick-lime is required to decompose 107 grams of ammonium chloride, and what will be the weight of the calcium chloride and water produced? What weight of ammonia gas will be evolved?

6. Ammonium chloride is heated with caustic soda, the resultant gas led into water, this solution neutralized with nitric acid, then evaporated to dryness, and heated in a test-tube until decomposed. Write the equations for the various steps of this process.

9.—Determination of the Composition of Ammonia.

1. Take a eudiometer, fill it with mercury, and invert over a small trough or saucer, also containing mercury. Heat some ammonium hydrate and pass 20 cc. of the gas into the eudiometer. Then pass electric sparks from an induction coil through the gas, taking care to have the current at high tension so as to increase the heating effect. When the gas no longer expands, pass 30 cc. of

pure oxygen into the eudiometer and explode. Depress the eudiometer so as to bring the mercury to the same level inside and outside; then note the volume of the gas remaining in it.

To what extent did the volume of the gas increase?

What did this increase show regarding the molecular change?

What reduction of volume took place when oxygen was introduced and a spark passed?

How much of this reduction was due to oxygen and how much to hydrogen going into combination?

Does any free hydrogen remain? Is any oxygen left?

How much hydrogen and how much nitrogen in 20 cc. of ammonia?

$$2NH_3 = 3H_2 + N_2.$$

Apply Avogadro's law to explain the change of volume.

How is it possible for a gas, as ammonia, to contain more than its own volume of another gas, as hydrogen?

CHAPTER XXVI.

PERCENTAGE COMPOSITION AND FORMULAS.

1.—To Calculate the Formula of a Compound when its Percentage Composition is known.

As soon as we have determined what elements are present in an unknown compound, and what their relative weights are, we can use this knowledge to construct a formula which will show the molecular composition of the substance. For instance, a gaseous compound may yield oxygen and nitrogen on analysis, but this does not settle what oxide of nitrogen it is.

Some examples worked out will make clear the methods of solution and the principles on which they are based

EXAMPLES.

1. A certain compound when analyzed yielded sodium 27%, nitrogen 16·5%, oxygen 56 5%. What is a formula for it? The percentages give the relative weights of the constituents in a unit weight of the compound; therefore the relative weights of the different kinds of atoms in a molecule of the compound. In a molecule of this substance, if the weight of the sodium atoms be represented by 27, that of the nitrogen will be 16½, and that of the oxygen 56½ We must next find the *relative numbers* of these atoms in the molecule. To do this the percentage weight must be divided by the atomic weight of the element.

$$\text{Sodium,} \quad 27 \div 23 = 1\ 17 \pm$$
$$\text{Nitrogen,} \quad 16 \div 14 = 1\text{·}17 \pm.$$
$$\text{Oxygen,} \quad 56\text{·}5 \div 16 = 3\text{·}5 \pm.$$

We now know that for every 1·17 atoms of sodium there are 1·17 atoms of nitrogen and 3 5 atoms of oxygen. These figures are not absolutely correct, but in practical work, errors of experiment render mathematical accuracy an impossibility. The next step will be to determine what *integral numbers* will express these ratios. To do this, we divide the smallest of the quotients obtained in the last operation into each of the others.

Thus, for sodium, $\frac{1.17}{1.17}=1$.

" nitrogen, $\frac{1.17}{1.17}=1$.

" oxygen, $\frac{3.5}{1.17}=3$.

This tells us that the numbers of atoms of sodium, nitrogen and oxygen are as 1, 1 and 3. Hence a formula for the compound is $NaNO_3$, or some multiple of this, $n(NaNO_3)$.

2. A compound gave on analysis 78·3% silver, 4·3% carbon, 17·4% oxygen. Find a formula for it.

SOLUTION.

$78\cdot3 \div 108 = \cdot725$; $4\cdot3 \div 12 = \cdot358$; $17\cdot4 \div 16 = 1\cdot09$.

$\cdot725 \div \cdot358 = 2\pm$

$\cdot358 \div \cdot358 = 1$

$1\cdot09 \div \cdot358 = 3\pm$.

There are, therefore, two atoms of silver to one of carbon to three of oxygen. Hence a formula for the substance is Ag_2CO_3. This is not necessarily the exact formula, because $Ag_4C_2O_6$ or $Ag_{2n}C_nO_{3n}$ would answer just as well, so far as the data of the question apply. There is an element left out in stating the problem which is necessary for an exact solution. This is the vapor density, which will be dealt with in another chapter (page 144). For present practice, the lowest number of atoms permissible may be taken as the proper formula, which is then said to be **empirical**.

DEFINITION.

An **empirical formula** expresses the proportions by weight in which the constituents of a substance unite to form it.

To solve all similar problems observe the following rule —

1. *Divide the percentage amount of each constituent element by its own atomic weight.*

2. *Divide each of the quotients thus found by the lowest of them, and the numbers obtained will express the proportional number of atoms of each element in the compound.*

2.—Exercises.

The following are percentage compositions of various substances; determine a formula for each.

1. Carbon, 42·86; oxygen, 57·14.
2. Hydrogen, 2·73; chlorine, 97·27.
3. Hydrogen, ·83; sodium, 19·17; sulphur, 26·66, oxygen, 53·33.
4. Sodium, 39·31, chlorine, 60·69.
5. Nitrogen, 82·35; hydrogen, 17·65
6. Phosphorus, 91·17; hydrogen, 8·83.
7. Carbon, 26·67; hydrogen, 2·22; oxygen, 71·11.
8. Carbon, 75, hydrogen, 25.
9. Carbon, 12, calcium, 40, oxygen, 48.

10 ·9 gram of a substance containing carbon, hydrogen and oxygen is found on analysis to yield ·24 gram of carbon and ·02 of hydrogen. Calculate its simplest formula

11. ·9 gram of a substance containing carbon, oxygen and hydrogen is found on analysis to yield ·06 of hydrogen and ·48 of oxygen. Calculate its simplest formula.

12. A portion of a substance is found on analysis to yield 36 gram of carbon, ·06 gram of hydrogen, and 48 gram of oxygen. Calculate its formula

3.—To Calculate Percentage Composition from the Formula.

Sometimes we are given the formula of a substance and are asked to calculate the percentage composition. This is easily done. Proceed as follows :—

Find the molecular weight of the compound by taking the sum of the atomic weights of its constituents, then divide this separately into the weights of the atoms of the different elements in the molecule.

EXAMPLE.

Calculate the percentage composition of sulphate of copper, $CuSO_4$.

Copper	63·5
Sulphur	32
Oxygen (16×4)	64
	159·5

If, by weight, there are in 159½ parts of sulphate of copper 63½ parts of copper, how many parts by weight of the metal will there be in 100 of sulphate.

159½ of sulphate yield   63½ of copper.

∴ 1 will yield .... $\dfrac{63½}{159½}$

and ∴ 100 will yield .. $\dfrac{63·5}{159·5} \times \dfrac{100}{1} = 39·81$ per cent.

The percentage of sulphur and oxygen in this compound may be found in the same way.

4.—Exercises.

What is the percentage composition of each of the following substances:—

1. Hydrogen oxide, H_2O.
2. Hydrogen chloride, HCl.
3. Ammonia, NH_3.
4. Magnesium sulphate, $MgSO_4$.
5. Calcium carbonate, $CaCO_3$.
6. Nitrate of hydrogen (nitric acid), HNO_3?

Calculate the percentage compositions of carbon monoxide, CO, and carbon dioxide, CO_2, and show from the results obtained that for equal weights of carbon there is twice as much oxygen in the CO_2 as in the CO.

Solve similar problems when (1) H_2O and H_2O_2, (2) N_2O and NO are the substances taken.

5.—Graphic and Rational Formulas

RATIONAL FORMULA.

A rational formula, besides expressing the proportions by weight in which the elements are united, attempts also to show the grouping within the molecule of a compound For example:—

$\left.\begin{array}{l}HO\\HO\end{array}\right\} SO_2$ is the rational formula for sulphuric acid,—that is, two hydroxyl molecules joined with sulphur dioxide.

GRAPHIC FORMULAS

Graphic formulas express more fully than rational ones the manner in which we suppose atoms to be associated in forming compounds For example, the graphic formula for water is H—O—H.

For nitric acid the empirical formula is HNO_3; the rational formula is $NO_2(OH)$, and the graphic formula,

$$\begin{array}{c} O \\ \| \\ N-O-H \\ \| \\ O \end{array}$$

In graphic formulas, the lines indicate the manner in which the valencies of each element are disposed of; thus, nitrogen is joined to the other elements by five links, oxygen by two, and hydrogen by one, nitrogen being a pentad in *ic* compounds and a triad in *ous* compounds. In the formula for water, oxygen is shown to be a diad because it has two combining powers joining it to the two atoms of hydrogen.

The graphic formula for sulphuric acid may be written

$$\begin{array}{c} \text{O—H} \\ | \\ \text{O}=\text{S}=\text{O} \\ | \\ \text{O—H} \end{array}$$

Sulphur has the valencies six and four in its *ic* and *ous* compounds respectively.

The graphic formulas for ammonium chloride, ammonium nitrate, copper sulphate, copper nitrate, are respectively:—

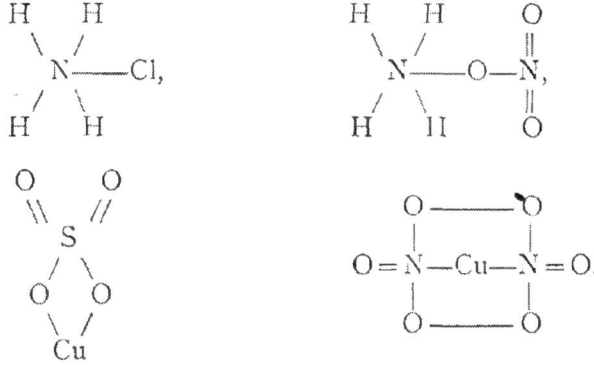

CHAPTER XXVII.

1.—Carbon.

OCCURRENCE.

Carbon is found in the free state, mixed with some impurities, as coal (chiefly lignite, bituminous coal and anthracite), as graphite or plumbago, and as diamonds. It also occurs very generally in combinations; for instance, it is a constituent of organic substances, both vegetable and animal; it enters into the composition of all carbonates, hence it forms one element in the limestones, both calcic and magnesic; it is found in soils and many minerals; and is a constituent of the hydrocarbons that make up petroleum and natural gas.

DEFINITION

The word **allotropism** is used to express the fact that some elements exist in very unlike states physically, or with very different properties, but preserve their fundamental chemical identity. See Chap. XII.

The allotropic forms of carbon are (1) **charcoal**, derived by roasting organic matters out of contact with air; (2) **graphite, plumbago,** or **black lead**, a mineral found chiefly in metamorphic rocks; and (3) **diamond**, a transparent crystalline variety of pure carbon.

2.—Experiments with Carbon.

1. Fit up apparatus, as in Fig. 29. In the left hand tube of hard-glass put dry fine shavings, or sawdust, and pass the delivery tube well under water, then heat the shavings strongly. Why does the wood not burn?

Does a gas come off? If so, will it burn?

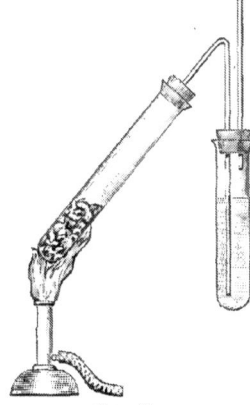
Fig. 29.

Does all the volatile material of the wood pass through the wash-water and escape at the outlet tube?

Test the wash-water with litmus. What conclusion?

Whether is the flame of the burning gas luminous or non-luminous?

Hold a cold dry plate or piece of metal in the flame. What is deposited?

Is the black deposit formed if the plate is held in the escaping gas when it is not burning?

Note the appearance and odor of the substance intercepted in the water.

When gas ceases to come off let the tube cool, spill out the contents, compare them with some of the original shavings.

Will the charcoal burn? Will it burn with a flame?

Dissolve the brown substance in the wash-tube with a little alcohol, pour it into an open dish and let the alcohol evaporate. Scrape up some of the residue on a wire and try if it will burn.

2. Repeat the experiment but heat white sugar instead of the wood.

In what respects do the results now agree with the former ones? Is there any noticeable difference?

3. Use some animal matter, as a bit of lean meat or a piece of woolen cloth, instead of the wood. Test the wash-water and the escaping gas with litmus.

Explanation.

When wood is roasted out of contact with air, (distilled), it yields (*a*) a solid residue, charcoal; (*b*) volatile products (1) easily condensible as tarry substances, (2) not easily condensible, as inflammable hydrocarbons. The volatile substances contain acid matters that are soluble.

Heat some soft coal in a hard-glass tube, as in Fig. 29, or in a retort fitted with a delivery tube. Wash the gas that comes off by letting it bubble through water.

Is the gas combustible? Test it with litmus.

Do any easily condensible substances pass over?

Judging by smell and appearance what is the yellow sticky substance in the water? Will it burn? What remained in the tube? What was intercepted by the wash-water? What passed into the air? Try the wash-water with Nessler's test for ammonia. Can ammonia be detected by the potash test?

4. Pass a solution of brown sugar two or three times through a filter made by coating a funnel with animal charcoal. Does the color of the solution change?

Evaporate a little of the solution after several filterings and compare the solid with the original. What kind of matter was removed by the charcoal?

3—Notes on Carbon.

Definition.

Roasting a substance out of contact with air is known as **destructive distillation** of it.

When organic matters are roasted the chemical compounds of which they are composed are broken up, just as in the case of wood, the volatile portions pass off as gases, some of which condense again at low temperatures, but others do not. That which remains as a solid is the carbon and contained minerals, the latter forming the ash when the charcoal is burned.

In preparation of illuminating gas soft coal is roasted in large retorts, the volatile substances are passed through water in which the ammonia and tarry ingredients are condensed, while the lighter gases pass on for further purification. The residue in the retort is coke or gas carbon. It is a valuable fuel as it comes from the retorts, and after being put through suitable processes some of it is made into such objects as electric light carbons, dynamo brushes, battery plates, etc. The coal tar obtained in the distillation for gas is chemically and industrially a substance of great importance. It is a mixture of many compounds; and from it is obtained such materials as paraffine, creosote, carbolic acid, picric acid, the aniline dyes, saccharine, benzine, pitch, etc. It is used in the manufacture of artificial fuels, in making roofing material and tarred papers, as a preservative for wood, metal and stone exposed to the weather, and as a material for road construction.

If the flame of a coal-oil lamp be turned too high it is said to *smoke*, and a black solid comes off in fine particles that are either deposited on the glass or escape into the air. A piece of paper saturated with turpentine or benzine and ignited, an alcohol lamp burning a solution of camphor, and a luminous gas flame with too little air supplied to it will all yield this same black, powdery solid called **soot** or **lampblack**. It is carbon set free from combinations usually with hydrogen (see page 156).

Carbon, then, is obtained artificially as lampblack, charcoal and coke. It occurs naturally as forming the larger part of the non-volatile substances in animal and vegetable tissues, and in peat, lignite, bituminous coal and anthracite. It exists in nature also as plumbago and diamond. It is combined mostly with hydrogen to form the mixture of substances known as petroleum and natural gas. It is also a constituent of that large class of salts called carbonates, many of them important rocks and minerals.

4.—Uses of Carbon.

Lampblack is chiefly used as a painter's color. Animal charcoal is largely employed in filtering operations in such places as sugar refineries and wine cellars, where it is desired to separate liquids from mechanically held, solid impurities. Wood charcoal is mostly employed as a fuel, especially in some industrial operations.

Coal of various kinds is so universally used for heating that no discussion is necessary regarding it. The warming of houses, the cooking of food, the reduction of ores, the furnishing of motive power in factories and on transportation lines, are all necessary factors in the life and civilization of modern times, and all are dependent on coal, and on that chemical property that it possesses of oxidizing readily and giving out a large amount of heat in the process

Graphite (plumbago) is used as a polishing material, as a lubricant for heavy machinery, in some electrical operations as a conductor, and as the *lead* of lead pencils.

5.— Questions and Exercises.

1. Charcoal is said to be an impure form of carbon. What impurities are found in it? Where do they come from?

2. Set fire to one corner of a sheet of paper and let it slowly burn away, then try if the charred sheet will again burn. What is finally left?

3. Water filters are frequently made of layers of sand and charcoal laid alternately. Is it likely that this would prove a serviceable arrangement? Would it be *permanently* effective?

4. Try to burn the lead of a lead pencil; also a piece of electric light carbon.

5. What is the source of the ashes produced in a coal fire?

Would one be likely to find ashes after burning coal-oil, coal tar, coal gas, lampblack?

6. For every ton of coal that is burned how much oxide of carbon is sent into the air, assuming that coal is 90% carbon and the chemical action is expressed by the equation $C + 2O = CO_2$?

CHAPTER XXVIII.

Carbon Compounds.

The chemical combinations of carbon are very numerous, so much so that one important branch of the science is devoted to them alone. No satisfactory study of the element can be made, however, without taking account of a few of these substances.

1.— Oxides of Carbon.

There are two well-known oxides of carbon, viz., carbon monoxide (carbonic oxide), CO, and carbon dioxide (carbonic anhydride, carbonic acid gas, or choke damp), CO_2. The latter is of general distribution in the atmosphere; and, dissolved in water, has played a very important part in the formation of the rocky crust of the earth. It is also necessary for the support of vegetable life.

2.—Carbon Dioxide.

The test for the presence of this gas is *limewater*. This is prepared by pouring water on lime, letting it stand for several hours, with frequent stirring, then allowing it to settle and decanting the clear liquid. This should have a distinctly alkaline taste, and should be free from turbidity. When carbon dioxide is passed through limewater a white precipitate is thrown down. Lime is oxide of calcium, CaO; dissolved in water it changes into a slightly soluble hydroxide, $Ca(HO)_2$, which is an alkaline base. CO_2 dissolved in water makes carbonic acid, H_2CO_3. This combines with the hydroxide to form calcium carbonate, $CaCO_3$, an insoluble white precipitate, $H_2CO_3 + Ca(HO)_2 = CaCO_3 + 2H_2O$.

EXPERIMENTS.

1. Twist one end of a piece of fine wire round a bit of charcoal, hold the latter in a lamp flame until it is glowing brightly, then lower it into a bottle and insert the cork beside the wire; when the charcoal ceases to burn withdraw it and shake up some limewater with the gas in the bottle. Contrive a means of driving the gas in the bottle through limewater in a test-tube.

2. Take the apparatus used in preparing hydrogen and place in it some powdered limestone or marble. Pour down the thistle-tube some dilute hydrochloric acid.

Collect, over water, some vessels full of the gas. **The** equation for the re-action is :—

$$CaCO_3 + 2HCl = CaCl_2 + H_2CO_3 \text{ ; and } H_2CO_3$$

at once decomposes into H_2O and CO_2, so that the products may be taken as $CaCl_2 + H_2O + CO_2$.

What appearance has the gas?

Will it burn?

Is it soluble?

Is it acid forming with water?

Will it support the combustion of a blazing splinter, of a candle, of burning phosphorus?

3. Put a little limewater in a flask, then try if CO_2 can be poured like water from another vessel into that flask.

Do not shake the flask, but watch for a white layer on the surface of the limewater.

What does this indicate as to the relative weights of air and carbon dioxide?

If one wanted to collect the gas without the use of water which way should the delivery tube be turned?

Vary the experiment by balancing an empty flask of at least a half litre (pint) capacity on a scale, then filling it with carbon dioxide gas. How may a person be sure when the vessel is full?

4. By using a piece of glass tubing pass the air exhaled from the lungs through limewater.

What happens?

Try if air forced through the tube for an equal length of time produces a similar result?

Point out any conclusion that these observations would warrant.

5. Invert a tube full of carbon dioxide over mercury, then with a curved pipette pass a solution of potassic hydrate up into the tube. Vary the experiment by trying to collect the gas over a solution of caustic potash. What is the result?

$CO_2 + H_2O = H_2CO_3$; and $H_2CO_3 + 2KHO = K_2CO_3 + 2H_2O$. K_2CO_3 is a readily soluble salt.

Give two ways by which carbon dioxide might be separated from air.

6. Is carbon dioxide given off by burning gas, burning alcohol, from a coal-oil lamp, from a blazing splinter?

3.—Carbonic Acid and Carbonates.

Carbon dioxide dissolved in water forms a solution of carbonic acid. This acid is a very weak one, it is easily displaced from its combinations, it cannot be separated from its solution without undergoing decomposition into oxides of hydrogen and carbon, yet it is the acid radical of a great number of important compounds that are generally stable. Calcium carbonate, for instance, takes the forms of bedded limestone, calcite, marble, chalk, animal shells, and marl. Carbonates of iron, lead, zinc, and barium are important minerals; magnesium carbonate is the chief material of dolomitic limestones; and carbonates of sodium, potassium and ammonium are largely used in industrial operations.

All carbonates are decomposed by the common mineral acids (nitric, hydrochloric, sulphuric) because these displace the carbonic acid of the salt, and it then breaks up into water and carbon dioxide gas, thus:—

$$MgCO_3 + H_2SO_4 = MgSO_4 + H_2CO_3$$
$$\text{and } H_2CO_3 = H_2O + CO_2.$$

The alkaline carbonates alone are soluble in water. Some carbonates when strongly heated break up into carbon dioxide and the oxide of the metal. The well-known burning of limestone to form lime serves as an example:

$$CaCO_3 = CaO + CO_2.$$

EXPERIMENTS.

1. Take a hydrogen generating apparatus and place in it some broken oyster shells. Then pour down the thistle-tube some hydrochloric acid. Collect the gas that escapes and test it for carbon dioxide.

Repeat the experiment using egg shells, snail shells, chalk (not blackboard crayons which are mostly plaster of Paris), calcite, washing soda, and some of the coating off the inside of a tea kettle.

2. Pass CO_2 into limewater until a thick ppt. forms, then add drop by drop some hydrochloric or nitric acid. When the ppt. has disappeared drop in some ammonia or caustic potash solution.

Assuming that hydrochloric acid has been used, the following equations express the re-actions. Translate the formulas into words:—

$$Ca(HO)_2 + CO_2 = CaCO_3 + H_2O.$$
$$CaCO_3 + 2HCl = CaCl_2 + H_2O + CO_2.$$

Try if moistened red litmus paper is changed to blue by limestone, marble or oyster shell.

Wind a bit of wire about the limestone and hold it in a flame until a coating of grey powder forms on the outside of it.

What effect has this powder on the litmus paper?

Does oyster shell undergo a similar change when heated? Does egg shell?

$$CaCO_3 = CaO + CO_2.$$

The CaO is lime and the CO_2 passes off as gas.

Does lime give off a gas when treated with an acid?

4. Mortar is made by mixing lime, sand and water

Procure some fresh (quick) lime and sand, mix them in about equal parts by weight, then add water enough to make a paste. Does this give off gas when treated with an acid? Then try if some old mortar from a building will act just in the same way with acid.

What result is noticeable?

What conclusion about the chemical composition of fresh and of old mortar?

What gas escaped?

What does it show?

5. Pass a current of carbon dioxide through a test-tube containing limewater for about ten minutes.

Did a precipitate form?

Did it continue?

Test the liquid with litmus. Is it still limewater?

Divide the liquid into several parts, and drop a little alkali, as sodium hydroxide or ammonia, into one, add more limewater to a second, boil a third.

If there was free acid in the solution what would be the effect of adding the alkali?

What effect would boiling have on carbonic acid?

6.—Notes on Carbon Dioxide, Carbonic Acid and the Carbonates.

Carbon dioxide : symbol, CO_2; mol. weight, 44; vapor density, 22; soluble to the extent of about 3 vols. of gas in 2 of water; exists in air to the extent of about 4 vols. in 10,000. This supply is maintained by the breath of animals, the combustion of carbonaceous matters, the decomposition of carbonates, and by fermentation.

This gas is the choke damp of miners; so named because of the formation of large quantities of it by the explosion of another gas (fire damp, page 149) in the mines, and its deadly effect when breathed continuously. As it contains no free oxygen it is incapable of supporting life, so asphyxiation results if it is inhaled for any length of time.

Very large quantities of this gas are set free by the burning of fuels, the breathing of animals and the decomposition of organic matters. On the other hand, it is absorbed extensively by plants. The green coloring matter in the cells of the leaves has the power, in sunlight, of decomposing the gas and appropriating the carbon to build up the cell structure, while part of the oxygen is set free.

Carbon dioxide is one of the gases always found in excess in ill-ventilated rooms. The normal mixture of this gas in the air is ·04 of one per cent, when this rises by respiration to ·08 of one per cent the air is reaching the limit at which it can be inhaled without injury. A man breathes out about 6 cub. ft of this gas per hour, and this would raise the mixture in 1,000 cub. ft. of air from ·04 of one per cent to 1 of one per cent, hence the need for the frequent change of air in inhabited rooms.

Mortar, when freshly made, is strongly alkaline, the atmosphere contains water vapor and carbon dioxide, the ingredients of carbonic acid, consequently there is a chemical action, very gradual though, by which the lime is changed, in part at least, from the oxide back into the carbonate. Of course, mortar dries in the early stages of its "setting" or hardening, but a chemical change also goes on.

When the carbon dioxide is first passed into the limewater a precipitate of calcic carbonate, $CaCO_3$, is thrown down; when the water becomes saturated with the dioxide this precipitate is dissolved; perhaps because of the formation of an acid carbonate, $CaH_2(CO_3)_2$; but any treatment that takes the carbon dioxide out of the solution causes the precipitate to be again formed, because water alone will not dissolve the neutral carbonate. Boiling expels the carbonic acid gas, and the alkaline hydrates unite with it to form other carbonates. Water, therefore, which contains carbon dioxide in solution is capable of dissolving limestone slightly, thus it helps to bring about disintegration of masses of that rock.

Natural waters, as of springs, that contain carbonates of calcium or magnesium in solution, because they first dissolved CO_2, are said to be *hard*. When such waters are boiled the CO_2 is expelled and the dissolved carbonate is deposited as a coating on the interior of the containing vessel. This is the origin of the brown or grey scale that forms on the inside of kettles and steam boilers. It is known as *fur*, and is objectionable because it lowers the conducting power of the vessel for heat. Engineers who are obliged to use such water for steam generation have to take measures to remove the fur to keep it from interfering with the efficiency of their boilers.

7.—Uses of Carbon dioxide and Carbonates.

The quantity of a gas held in solution by a liquid may be increased by lowering the temperature and increasing the pressure. Advantage is taken of this principle in the preparation of effervescing drinks which generally have as their bases a solution of carbon dioxide in water. The gas is obtained artificially by the action of sulphuric acid on sodium carbonate.

In fermented drinks, as ales and wines, the gas is generated within the liquid by the growth of a vegetable organism, the yeast plant or a similar ferment, that in its life process gives off CO_2.

One of the most common applications of any chemical compound to ordinary operations is the use of carbon dioxide in bread-making. The starch and gluten of the flour, when mixed with water, would make a mass entirely too solid for comfortable consumption, so a means has been found for preventing this solidification by setting free countless bubbles of gas in the mass of dough. Sometimes ammonium salts are used for this purpose, but the more general plan is to generate carbon dioxide in the mass. This is done chiefly in two ways: either by sowing yeast plants within the dough, then securing conditions, chiefly of temperature and moisture, that promote rapid growth of the ferment, and thus produce a general distribution of gas, that, by its internal pressure causes expansion (*rising*) of the sponge or dough; or by the use of chemicals, chiefly baking powders, that, when moistened, interact to form a soluble salt and carbon dioxide. In either case the working or kneading of the dough drives the gas bubbles throughout the mass, thus securing a greater division of parts. At the proper stage the sponge is heated, and the dough encircling the bubbles of gas becomes fixed in its position at the same time that the materials are cooked, and the indigestible starchy material changed into digestible forms.

Carbonates are of considerable industrial importance. Some are valuable ores, as carbonates of iron and copper. Limestone is too well-known as building material to require more than mention, and its use for preparation of lime has been already referred to. In the form of marble it is employed in ornamental stone work largely. Magnesium carbonate serves purposes similar to those of the calcium compounds, except in the manufacture of lime. Lead carbonate is the white lead which painters use; and carbonates of the alkaline metals are largely employed in cleansing compounds and in manufacturing operations.

8.—Reducing power of Carbon.

Carbon is very largely used in metallurgy as a reducing agent, the monoxide and dioxide being formed in the process. The following experiments illustrate the principle on which it acts:—

1. Mix in a hard glass tube, closed at one end, some copper oxide and powdered charcoal; on top of this place a thick layer of charcoal, then heat strongly. Test the gas coming off for oxides of carbon. Examine what remains in the tube.

2. Repeat the preceding experiment but use arsenic trioxide for copper oxide. What appears on the cold part of the tube?

3. Try if red lead and iron rust are changed, when subjected to treatment similar to that applied to the copper oxide.

EXPLANATION.

We have already found that some compounds, as HgO, and Pb_3O_4, undergo reduction by heating alone. Possibly this method might be more general if a high enough temperature could be economically secured; but as that is not practicable, resort must be had to reducing agents, that is, substances that will form chemical combinations with the non-metallic elements of the compounds. Hydrogen has already been found to be effective for this purpose, but it is too expensive to be used on a large scale for ore reduction. The smelting of an iron ore, hematite, Fe_2O_3, for instance, illustrates the general principle. A circular iron furnace, usually in the form of two cones placed base to base, is carried to a height of sixty to eighty feet and lined with a thick coating of fire clay to protect the wall plates. At the base are appliances for controlling the fire, for supplying air as needed and for drawing off slag and molten iron. The furnace is filled with alternate layers of coal, iron ore and limestone, the latter for the absorption of impurities in the ore. When filled the furnace is lighted by starting a fire in its base which by forced draft is carried up through the mass. As the coal burns a very high temperature is produced; and part, at least, of the oxygen required for combustion is taken from the ore; the iron, fused by the great heat, trickles to the bottom of the furnace and is allowed to escape at intervals through a vent provided for it. The limestone also fuses and runs to the bottom as slag in combination with impurities it takes up; while the carbon oxidizes to CO and escapes at the mouth of the furnace.

9.—Questions and Exercises.

1. Devise experiments to show that coal gas and coal oil contain carbon as one of their constituents.

2. Twenty-five grams of sodium carbonate is heated with just enough hydrochloric acid to complete the chemical action; the gas that comes off is passed into solution of ammonia which is afterwards evaporated to dryness.
   (a) Write the equation for the re-action.
   (b) What weight of acid would be required? (Ordinary hydrochloric acid may be assumed to be a 20% solution by weight of the gaseous acid in water.)
   (c) What weight of each of the salts would be formed?

3. Mention substances that when burned do not yield carbonic acid gas as one of the products of combustion.

4. Is chalk dust soluble in water? Is sodium carbonate soluble in water? Why is a solution of calcium hydrate rather than a solution of sodium hydrate used as the test for carbon dioxide?

5. Why should engineers prefer rain water to spring water for use in steam boilers?

6. Try whether you can syphon carbon dioxide from one jar to another. Fill the tube with water at the start.

140 CARBON MONOXIDE, OR CARBONIC OXIDE.

7. Carbon dioxide led through a tube over slices of sodium or pieces of magnesium wire may be decomposed by heating the metal to redness. The oxygen of the CO_2 will go to form oxide of the metal, and carbon will be left as black particles that may be separated by gently washing.

8. A bottle holding 10 litres was filled with water which was emptied into other vessels in a school class room; 50 cc. of lime-water were immediately put into the bottle, and it was then tightly stoppered and shaken at intervals for a couple of hours. A filter paper had meantime been dried and weighed, the liquid in the bottle was washed out on this paper, and it was again dried and weighed. The difference in weight was 0·066 grams. What percentage of CO_2 was in the air of that room?

9. Given some baking soda, $NaHCO_3$, some sulphuric acid and some ammonia solution, explain how some ammonium carbonate might be prepared.

10. 22·4 litres of CO_2 weigh 44 grams, 22·4 litres of hydrogen weigh 2 grams, air is 14·4 times as heavy as hydrogen. How heavy is CO_2 as compared with air?

11. How may the flame of burning pine shavings be accounted for? Why is it that no tar is found when pine wood is burned? How is the formation of soot in a chimney or stove pipe after burning soft wood explained?

10.—Carbon Monoxide, or Carbonic Oxide.

EXPERIMENTS.

1. Into a Florence flask put 8 or 10 grams of oxalic acid, and about 50 cc. of sulphuric acid. Fit with a tight cork and tube and attach, as in Fig. 30, to a wash bottle containing a strong solution of caustic potash. From the wash bottle, a delivery tube should pass to the pneumatic trough. Apply heat cautiously to the

flask, regulating it so that the gas may come off in a slow, steady stream. After the air has been expelled from the apparatus, collect several bottles of gas, and allow them to stand over water for some time. Meanwhile, substitute for the delivery tube one whose end has been drawn to a fine point. Apply a lighted match to the jet.

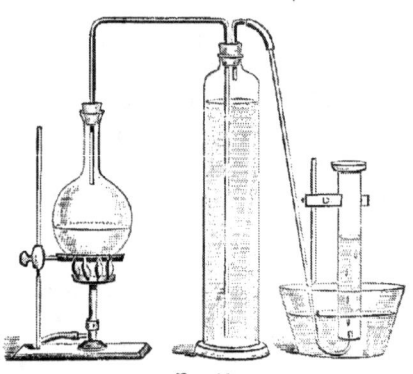

Fig. 30.

2. Raise one of the bottles of gas from the water, and apply a lighted taper to its mouth. How does the gas burn? What is the color of the flame?

3. Try to pour the gas from one bottle to another, then test the result with a lighted taper.

4. Purify thoroughly the gas in a third bottle, by shaking it up well with caustic potash or caustic soda solution, then test the gas with clear limewater. Ignite it and repeat the test. What is the conclusion?

EXPLANATION.

Carbon monoxide may also be obtained quite easily by heating ferrocyanide of potash (yellow prussiate of potash) $K_4FeC_6N_6$ with sulphuric acid somewhat diluted. In this case the gas may come off with a rush, so, free delivery should be provided for it. $K_4FeC_6N_6 + 6H_2SO_4 + 6H_2O = 2K_2SO_4 + FeSO_4 + 3(NH_4)_2SO_4 + 6CO$.

By this method there is no need to wash the gas in caustic potash solution unless it is required quite free from impurity.

When CO is prepared from oxalic acid advantage is taken of the avidity of sulphuric acid for water. This property of the acid may be shown by dropping a little of it on some white sugar or starch in a dish, and by throwing a piece of wood into some of the acid. Each of these substances consists of carbon, oxygen and hydrogen; the last two present in the proportions in which they are in water (sugar is $C_{12}H_{22}O_{11}$, starch is $C_6H_{10}O_5$, woody tissue is largely cellulose, $C_6H_{10}O_5$ also); from these the acid absorbs the elements of water, thus leaving carbon Sulphuric acid acts in a similar way with many organic compounds, such as oxalic acid, $C_2H_2O_4$, thus, $C_2H_2O_4 + H_2SO_4 = H_2SO_4 + H_2O + CO + CO_2$. The washing in caustic potash is to get rid of the dioxide.

The two oxides of carbon are easily converted one into the other by oxidation or reduction, thus CO will burn readily in air with a characteristic blue flame to CO_2; and CO_2 passed through red-hot carbon is reduced to CO. Thus, in an ordinary coal stove, air entering through the front damper changes part of the coal first met with to CO_2, but as this gas passes up through hot coal in the fire pot it loses part of its carbon and becomes CO, thus, $CO_2 + C = 2CO$. At the top of the fire, if the gas comes into contact with a free supply of air, it again undergoes oxidation to CO_2.

The blue flame that plays over the top of a bright fire when fresh coal is thrown on it is due to burning monoxide of carbon which is probably produced by the dust of the coal undergoing rapid combustion where there is not sufficient oxygen to complete the burning, consequently when a larger supply of air is met the oxidation to the higher product is finished.

In general, when carbon burns in a limited supply of oxygen the monoxide is formed; but if there is plenty of oxygen the dioxide is produced. Carbon monoxide is poisonous so should not be inhaled.

11—Uses of Carbon Monoxide.

In ore smelting, it was formerly the custom to allow the carbonic oxide to burn out at the mouth of the furnace. In modern practice this waste has been eliminated by collecting the gas before it oxidizes to CO_2 and leading it away to be used for heating purposes in other parts of the works.

One kind of illuminating gas, often called *water gas*, is manufactured by blowing jets of steam through a mass of white-hot coal. The chemical action is indicated by the equation $C + H_2O = CO + H_2$ The mixture of carbon monoxide and hydrogen thus formed has high heating power, but it has not great luminosity. This defect is made good by mixing the gas with others rich in hydrocarbons; these are generally obtained from crude petroleum.

12.—Questions and Exercises.

1. Will carbonic oxide and oxygen explode in a eudiometer when a spark is passed?

2. On what data can one conclude that carbon dioxide contains more oxygen than carbon monoxide?

3. Thirty grams of oxalic acid is treated with excess of sulphuric acid, the resultant gas led through a solution of sodium hydrate in which all the carbon dioxide is dissolved, the remaining gas is burned, and the product of combustion passed into limewater where it unites with the dissolved hydrate. Write equations for the several re-actions, and determine what weight of each compound is formed.

4. In what particulars (3 at least) does hydrogen resemble carbon monoxide? How would you distinguish them, if similar jars were filled, one with each gas?

CHAPTER XXIX.

1.—Density of Gases.

Formerly air was the standard with which other gases were compared in the matters of density and weight. Now hydrogen is almost always used for that purpose. Any determination may be easily reduced from one basis to the other by remembering that air is 14 4 times as heavy as hydrogen.

Density of a gas is the mass in a unit volume, and, since mass is expressed in terms of weight, densities are expressed by the weights of unit volumes.

The following two principles are important:—

(1) *The density of a gas is expressed by a number equal to one half its molecular weight, ($H = 1$).*

DEMONSTRATION.

By Avogadro's law, equal volumes of gases under like conditions of temperature and pressure contain equal numbers of molecules. Suppose that a unit volume of a gas, G, contains x molecules, then a unit volume of hydrogen also contains x molecules. Suppose, further, that W is the molecular weight of the gas G. Then the unit volume of G weighs W × x, while the unit volume of hydrogen weighs 2 × x, since the molecular weight of hydrogen is 2. Then for equal volumes the gas G weighs $\frac{Wx}{2x} = \frac{W}{2}$ times as much as hydrogen; but W is the molecular weight of the gas, hence it is $\frac{W}{2}$ times as heavy as hydrogen, or its density = ½W, (H = 1)

(2) *22.4 litres of a gas at standard temperature and pressure weigh that number of grams expressed by its molecular weight.*

DEMONSTRATION.

By experiment 22.4 (22.36 to be more accurate) litres of hydrogen weigh 2 grams. If W = the molecular weight of a gas, G, then 22.4 litres of that gas weigh ½W times as much as an equal volume of hydrogen, or ½W × 2 grams = W grams, but W is the mol. weight of the gas, hence 22.4 litres of it weigh the number of grams expressed by its molecular weight.

This is much used in translating weights into volumes and *vice versa*, so should be quite familiar.

It will be well to keep in mind two physical laws that affect the volume of a fixed weight of a gas, and must, therefore, be taken into account in all calculations, except when the standard conditions of temperature and pressure exist. These laws are BOYLE'S and CHARLES'. The former relates to pressure and tells us that, when temperature is constant, the volume of a quantity of gas confined in a closed vessel varies inversely as the pressure to which it is subjected. The latter relates to temperature, and according to it the volume of a quantity of gas under a constant pressure varies as the absolute temperature, the absolute temperature of O°C being 273°C. If a quantity of gas occupied 'a' vols. at pressure x, and if the pressure changed to 'y,' the volume would then be $a \times \dfrac{x}{y}$; also if the absolute temperature at first was t°C, then if this changed to p°C, the correction would be obtained by using the factor $\dfrac{p}{t}$. The final volume will, therefore, be $a \times \dfrac{x}{y} \times \dfrac{p}{t}$.

2.—Questions and Exercises.

Assume standard temperature and pressure, unless others are given

1. How many grams of hydrogen will occupy 224 litres at the standard temperature and pressure?

2. Steam is passed through a tube containing red-hot iron filings, 18 litres of hydrogen pass out at the other end. What volume of steam was decomposed, and how much are the iron filings increased in weight? Assume temperature and pressure constant.

3. How much sulphuric acid and zinc must be taken to form 112 litres of hydrogen at 7°C?

4. In 285 grams of caustic potash how many grams of potassium? How many of hydrogen?

5. What weight of sodium must be taken to obtain 20 grams of hydrogen from a litre of water? If temperature were raised to 70° C and pressure to 800 mm., what would the volume of the

QUESTIONS AND EXERCISES.   147

hydrogen then be? How much sodium would be needed to get 20 litres at this temperature and pressure?

6. A reservoir of hydrogen gas holds 89.6 litres. What weight of water will be formed by burning the gas in air? What volume of air will be required for the combustion, assuming that it is 21%, by volume, oxygen?

7. 25 litres of oxygen are exploded with 36 of hydrogen. What volume of gas (if any) remains? What volume of steam is produced at 100°C? And what is its weight? Does the weight change when temperature is raised to 120°? Does the mass alter with temperature or with pressure?

8. If 10 litres of carbon dioxide be passed over red-hot charcoal, what gas, and how many litres of it, will be formed at 30°C? What weight of it?

9. 20 litres of carbonic oxide are burned in oxygen gas. What gas is produced, what volume at 40°C and what weight of it?

10. How much carbon can be obtained from 264 grams of carbon dioxide? Would change of pressure vary the answer?

11. What volume of oxygen at 10°C is required to burn 66 grams of carbon? How would the volume of the gas formed compare with that of the oxygen used?

12. How can it be demonstrated that carbon is a constituent of limestone and of washing soda?

13. A mixture of nitrogen and hydrogen occupied 18 cc. in a eudiometer over mercury; oxygen was introduced to make 31 cc; a spark was then passed and the mercury rose to the 13th division of the scale; how much hydrogen was in the mixture and how much nitrogen?

CHAPTER XXX.

CARBON AND HYDROGEN.

1.—Methane.

Methane (Marsh Gas, Light Carburetted Hydrogen "Fire-damp"), CH_4; molecular weight, 16, vapor, density, 8.

EXPERIMENTS

1. Take a hard glass test-tube or Florence flask and fit it with a cork and fine delivery tube (a copper retort used for preparation of oxygen is preferable as there is no danger of breaking it). Heat in the test-tube 4 grams of acetate of sodium, $NaC_2H_3O_2$, 8 grams of sodium hydroxide, and 4 grams of finely-powdered quicklime, CaO. After collecting a beaker or two of the gas, light the jet and observe the color of the flame

Before lighting the gas, test it in the same way as hydrogen to see that it is not mixed with air.

Hold a cold plate just above the flame and examine it for moisture.

Collect a little of the product of the combustion and test it with limewater.

In the combustion what was derived from the air?

What other elements must have been present to give the results observed?

What conclusion about the constituents of marsh gas?

METHANE.

The formula for the re-action in the preparation of the gas is

(1) $NaC_2H_3O_2 + Ca(HO)_2 = CaCO_3 + NaHO + CH_4$

(2) $NaC_2H_3O_2 + NaHO = Na_2CO_3 + CH_4$.

hence:

(3) $2NaC_2H_3O_2 + Ca(HO)_2 = Na_2CO_3 + CaCO_3 + 2CH_4$.

2. Fill a small soda water bottle with a mixture of one part of the gas and two parts of oxygen. Ignite the mixture. Express the re-action by an equation.

3. Take a stoppered bottle and fill it with a mixture of equal volumes of marsh gas and chlorine. Expose to sunlight for a day, then test the contents with blue litmus Note any change in color.

EXPLANATION.

Methane is generated in marshes by the decomposition of vegetable matter containing carbon and hydrogen. It may be secured in the late autumn by stirring the dead leaves in ponds and directing the bubbles of gas through an inverted funnel into a bottle. It is found also in coal mines, filling seams and pockets; as the miners open these up, the gas escapes, and, on being mixed with air it is liable to become ignited from the workmen's lights and produce very dangerous explosions, hence, in miners' language, it is "fire damp." To prevent these accidents Sir H. Davy invented his celebrated **Safety Lamp.**

Methane is the first of a series of hydrocarbons known as the marsh gas series. Each member of it differs from the following one by the group CH_2. All are inflammable. The general formula for the series is C_nH_{2n+2}.

2.—Olefiant Gas

Ethylene (Ethene. Olefiant gas. Heavy carburetted hydrogen), C_2H_4, molecular weight, 28, vapor density, 14. The general formula of this series is C_nH_{2n}.

EXPERIMENTS.

1 Into a Florence flask pour 50 or 60 cc. of strong sulphuric acid and half that volume of alcohol. Insert a tightly-fitting cork and delivery tube. Place the flask on a retort stand and heat gently. After the air has all been expelled, collect two or three jars of the gas.

Alcohol has the formula C_2H_6O. The sulphuric acid acts here in the same way that it does on oxalic acid in the preparation of carbonic oxide, viz., by extracting the elements of water.

$$C_2H_6O + H_2SO_4 = C_2H_4 + H_2SO_4 + H_2O.$$

2. Ascertain whether the gas will burn or not Does it contain hydrogen? Is there carbon in it? Will it explode when mixed with oxygen? Is it soluble?

3.—Acetylene.

Acetylene, another hydrocarbon that has the formula C_2H_2, is of great economic importance for illuminating purposes, because of a recently-discovered method by which it can be produced at small expense in large quantites When calcium carbonate and powdered coal are heated in an electric furnace, calcium carbide, CaC_2, is formed This, when immersed in water, yields acetylene, and the gas burns with great luminosity in the air, when ignited at suitable jets The products of the re-action by which acetylene is formed are calcium hydrate and acetylene, thus :—

$$CaC_2 + 2H_2O = C_2H_2 + Ca(OH)_2.$$

ACETYLENE.

EXPERIMENTS.

1. Collect a gas jar full of acetylene by slipping a piece of calcium carbide under it on a plate of water.

What appearance has the gas?

Is it soluble?

Ignite the gas at the mouth of the jar and observe the character of the flame.

What is its color?

Where does the black soot come from?

If the composition of the gas is C_2H_2, what is it that chiefly burns?

What would be necessary to prevent soot forming when acetylene is burned?

2. Repeat the experiment, but fill the gas jar something more than half full of oxygen (air may be used, but the jar should be filled at least three quarters full of it), before the carbide is passed in. When the jar is full hold the mouth of it to a flame. How does the result of the burning in this case differ from the former one (*a*) in the manner of burning, (*b*) in the products of combustion?

3. Use a stoppered gas jar (a thick-walled bottle with the bottom cut off will answer very well) and fill it with acetylene; take out the stopper, ignite the gas at the top, then lift the jar out of water while the burning goes on.

Why is there an explosion?

Will coal gas act in a similar way?

4. Employ the jar of the last experiment, but insert a blow-pipe nozzle in a hole in the cork to serve as a jet,

and have the jar standing in a deep vessel, so that by pressing it down into the water the gas may be driven out of the jet. Ignite the escaping gas.

How is the luminosity of the flame affected?

What is the improvement in light-giving properties due to?

CHAPTER XXXI.

COAL GAS AND FLAME.

1.—Coal Gas

The average composition of coal gas (for it is really a mixture of many gases) is about as follows.—

Hydrogen	45
Marsh gas	35·
Carbonic oxide	7·
Olefiant gas	4·
Butylene	2·4
Hydric sulphide	0·3
Nitrogen	2·5
Carbon dioxide	3·8
Total	100· vols.

When the gas comes from the retort it contains a much larger quantity of hydrogen sulphide, carbon dioxide and ammonia. In the purifying processes these are separated. Any ingredient of coal gas which either does not burn with a luminous flame, or does not help to support the combustion of the other substances, or forms offensive products in burning, is objectionable, and should be got rid of, if possible. Hydrogen sulphide will burn readily, but it yields sulphur dioxide, a very undesirable substance to have escaping into the air in dwellings.

2 —Luminosity of Flame.

EXPERIMENTS.

1. Sprinkle into the flame of an alcohol lamp or Bunsen burner some fine, solid particles, as iron filings, siftings from a blackboard eraser, or ground charcoal.

What change is noticeable in the particles that drop into the flame?

What becomes of the charcoal powder? What of the chalk? Would the light-giving power of the flame be affected by a shower of these solid particles? Why?

2. Hold a piece of platinum wire or a piece of lime in the flame of hydrogen gas.

Is the hydrogen flame a light-giving one?

Is the incandescent wire luminous?

What is the light due to?

3. Hold a cold plate horizontally in the flame of an alcohol lamp for a minute, then blow out the flame and put into the lamp about one half as much spirits of turpentine as there is of alcohol, quickly light the lamp and observe the change that comes over the character of the flame; again hold the cold plate in it.

What alteration did the flame undergo?

Why did it not occur at the moment of lighting?

To find a cause for the change try the following:—

Tear a piece of paper in two, dip one of the parts in alcohol, set fire to it and watch the flame. Saturate the other part with turpentine and ignite it. What difference is noticeable in combustion in the two cases?

Does any solid matter escape in either case? What would be the probable effect on the light given out if these solid particles were made incandescent?

Were there solid particles in the flame of mixed alcohol and turpentine?

Why did the flame become luminous?

Does the gas flame from an ordinary fish-tail burner contain solid particles? Can they be seen? Are they to be found in the flame of a coal-oil lamp?

Would coal oil or benzine do to mix with the alcohol instead of turpentine?

Try what effect some camphor gum put into the lamp has on the luminosity of an alcohol flame

4. Open the holes at the base of a lighted Bunsen burner. Try, by using smoke, if there is a current of air entering these holes. Unscrew the tube and observe the location of the gas vent.

What passes out at the top of the tube (1) when the holes are closed; (2) when the holes are open?

How is oxygen supplied for the combustion (1) when the holes are open, (2) when they are closed?

5. Close the holes at the base of a Bunsen burner, turn on the gas and light it. What kind of flame is there? Turn off the gas and invert a common funnel over the burner, as in Fig 31, still leaving the holes at the base closed; turn on the gas and after a few seconds light it at the end of the funnel stem. What sort of a flame is there now? Why?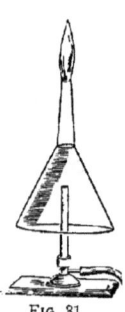

FIG. 81

3 —Structure of Flame.

1. Spread out the wick of a candle or alcohol lamp, light it, and then thrust into the middle of the flame the phosphorus end of a match.

Similarly pass the end of a match into the cone of gas in the middle of the non-luminous flame of a Bunsen burner.

Repeat the experiment, with both lamp and burner, but insert the match half way between the bottom and top of the flame.

What is the conclusion about the temperatures of these parts of the flame?

Is the flame hotter towards the exterior?

2. Bring a piece of wire gauze down horizontally upon the flame of an alcohol lamp, or a Bunsen burner.

What conclusion may be drawn from the way in which the gauze gets hot as to where temperature is highest in a flame?

3. Light a candle and observe its flame carefully. Note (1) the dark central mass surrounding the wick;

FIG. 32.

(2) the highly luminous middle portion; (3) the yellowish gray outer mantle scarcely at all light-giving. Take a narrow bent glass tube, about four or five inches long, and thrust one end of it into the dark cone in the middle of the flame, as in Fig. 32. Try to light the vapors which rise through the tube. Repeat the experiment, but use a Bunsen burner instead of the candle. Try, both when the holes at the base are open and when they are closed.

4. Pass a sheet of white paper horizontally across the flame of a candle at different heights; hold it at each place a moment until the paper chars, but remove it before it ignites. What conclusions may be drawn from the charred marks about the structure of a flame? Do the flames of an alcohol lamp and of a gas burner give similar results.

EXPLANATION.

Substances that are burned for illuminating purposes consist mostly of hydrocarbons; and when these are in the solid or the liquid form at ordinary temperatures, they are changed into gases by the application of heat. In the case of a candle, for instance, the solid matter is melted and the liquid is drawn up through the wick and vaporized by the heat of the flame.

At the temperature of the lower part of the flame the compounds that contain most hydrogen are partly decomposed, that element being set free. This hydrogen combines with the oxygen that is in contact with the mass of burning gas, and by its union raises the temperature still higher, entirely decomposing the remaining hydrocarbons. The burning hydrogen heats the carbon to incandescence; but, as oxygen has not access to the interior body of the flame the carbon does not burn until it is carried to the outer parts of the flame. The luminosity of the flame is due to incandescent particles of solid carbon, the necessary heat being produced mostly by burning hydrogen, set free from these very carbon particles.

There are generally three mantles or cones in a candle flame (an alcohol lamp with turpentine will also illustrate this); (1) the cone of unburning gas in the middle next the wick, (2) the incandescent mantle in which carbon particles are heated to whiteness but are not consumed for lack of oxygen, (3) the outer mantle faintly luminous, in which the carbon is burned to CO_2.

If air be mixed with the gas so that there is plenty of oxygen to complete the combustion, the solid particles burn up without becoming incandescent and the flame is non-luminous. If the burning gas contains little or no carbon, as hydrogen; or if it contains oxygen which will combine with the carbon when the hydrogen is set free, as alcohol, C_2H_6O, the flame will not be a light-giving one.

4.—Questions and Exercises.

1. Mention one way of changing a non-luminous flame into a luminous one.

2. Explain the source of the black mark formed on a white plate by holding it horizontally across the flame of a candle, or of a coal-oil lamp. What is the black substance?

3. Turpentine is $C_{10}H_{16}$, benzine C_6H_6, camphor $C_{10}H_{16}O$. Does this composition explain in any way the luminosity imparted to a flame when one of these substances is introduced into it?

4. Make a small cone-shaped helix of copper wire and invert it over a candle flame.

Does burning gas come through the spaces between the wires?

Make the helix red hot, then invert it over the flame again.

What is the result this time?

What effect is produced on a flame by cooling the mass of gas?

Why did the copper wire put the flame out?

5. Hold a piece of fine brass wire gauze, such as tinsmiths use in making strainers, about an inch above the top of a Bunsen burner, turn on the gas and light it above the gauze.

Why does the gas not take fire at once on the under side of the gauze?

Why does it ignite later?

In the "Safety Lamp," invented by Davy and used by coal miners, the flame is entirely surrounded by a wire gauze cylinder closed at the top, so that there may not be heat enough to ignite the fire damp, CH_4, outside the gauze. How is this rise of temperature prevented? Read about this lamp.

6. How many volumes of oxygen would be required to complete the combustion to carbon dioxide and water of each of the following,—10 volumes of hydrogen, 10 volumes of carbonic oxide, 10 volumes of marsh gas, and 10 volumes of olefiant gas?

7. A mixture of hydrogen and carbonic oxide, obtained by blowing jets of steam into white-hot coals, is used as an illuminant,

and is known technically as water gas (to distinguish it from coal gas obtained by the distillation of coal). Explain the chemical re-actions, with equations, that go on in the preparation of this gas. The constituents of this gas are not sufficiently light-giving, so it has to be enriched by the introduction of carbon; some of the gases driven off from crude oil, (petroleum) by heating are mixed with the others for this purpose.

8. Why is the burner of a gas jet made with an opening in the form of a slit instead of a round hole? and why is an argand burner made to allow air to pass up the middle of it?

9. Use a two-necked Woulff's jar as a hydrogen generator, arrange it as shown in Fig. 33, putting a plug of cotton wool in the wide tube; after all the air is driven out set fire to the hydrogen escaping from both tubes. Remove the stopper from the large tube, pour two or three drops of benzine (C_6H_6) on the cotton, replace the stopper and again ignite the gas. How is the change accounted for?

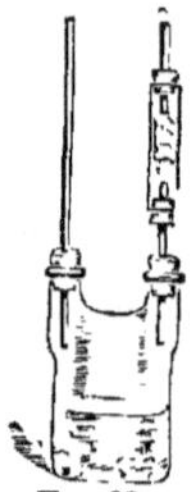

Fig 33.

10. "Soft coal" or bituminous coal burns with a bright luminous flame, "hard coal" or anthracite glows, and burns away almost entirely without flame. Why is there a difference?

11. A lamp flame turned too high will smoke; of what does this smoke consist? Whence does it come? Why is it formed only when the flame is turned too high? What are the clouds of black smoke that come out of factory chimneys? If this smoke escapes most freely just after fresh coal has been put on the fire, how is its formation explained? What does the "burning of smoke" in factories mean?

12. When wood was roasted in a tube, the escaping gas was thick with smoke until it was ignited, then the smoke disappeared. Why?

13. When a candle flame is blown out, how is the chemical action made to cease?

5.—Blowpipe Flame.

Three zones are observed when a flame has a jet of air blown into it from the nozzle of a blowpipe. The inner mantle or zone of incomplete combustion, R, Fig. 34, is technically known as the *reducing flame*, because here the supply of oxygen is limited, hence the carbon has been oxidized only to carbonic oxide, and there is, therefore, a great tendency to take oxygen away from

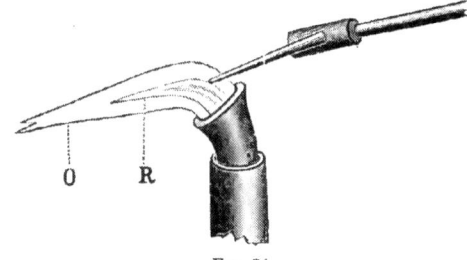

Fig. 34.

any substance that will part with it. The outer mantle, O, is the *oxidizing* flame, because the supply of oxygen is plentiful, and the heating of a substance to a high degree in contact with oxygen, of course promotes chemical union between the two, if that is possible.

CHAPTER XXXII.

CHLORINE.

1.—The Halogens.

There are four elements—chlorine, bromine, iodine, and fluorine—that are closely related to one another, and are known in chemistry as *halogens* (salt producers). Chlorine is the most important of these. They all form acids that do not contain oxygen; these are sometimes called *haloid acids*, and the salts which they form, *haloid salts;* they are thus distinguished from salts and acids which contain oxygen.

2.—Experiments with Chlorine.

1. Put into a test-tube one part of manganese dioxide, two parts of salt, and three of sulphuric acid. Fit the test-tube with a cork and delivery tube. Heat gently and pass the gas that comes off into a dry receiver.

What is its color?

Smell it cautiously; what odor has it?

Is it soluble? Will it burn? Does a blazing splinter burn in it? Does it affect litmus?

EXPLANATION.

The preparation of the gas in this way turns on the displacement of hydrochloric acid from chlorides by sulphuric acid, then the oxidation of the hydrochloric acid by the peroxide present, MnO_2.

$$NaCl + H_2SO_4 = NaHSO_4 + HCl.$$
$$2HCl + MnO_2 + H_2SO_4 = MnSO_4 + 2H_2O + 2Cl.$$

These may be combined into—

$$2NaCl + MnO_2 + 3H_2SO_4 = MnSO_4 + 2NaHSO_4 + 2Cl.$$

If these re-actions go on together, there are being produced at the same time nascent oxygen, hydrogen and chlorine, of these the oxygen and hydrogen unite and the chlorine remains free.

2. To prepare the gas on a larger scale one may use commercial hydrochloric acid and by heating it and manganese dioxide together chlorine is evolved. Use fittings similar to those in Fig. 35. Apply a *very* gentle heat. The delivery tube should pass almost to the bottom of the jar. The decomposition is $4HCl + MnO_2 = MnCl_2 + 2H_2O + 2Cl$. Collect several vessels full of the gas, and place a wetted glass or paper over the mouth of each.

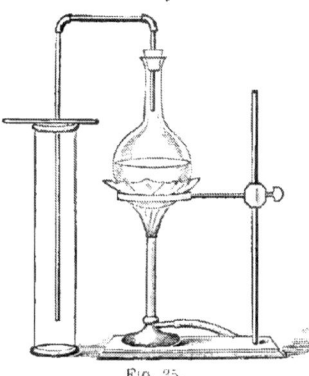

Fig. 35.

3. Lower very slowly a lighted taper into a jar of chlorine. How does the flame change in appearance?

Hydrogen combines readily with chlorine, carbon does not. Why should there be soot?

Test with blue litmus to find if an acid is formed. Does chlorine support combustion?

4. Rub some antimony to a fine powder, then shake this into a jar of chlorine. The white fumes are antimony trichloride, $SbCl_3$.

Lower some phosphorus in a chalk cup into another vessel of the gas. PCl_3 is formed in this case.

5. Make a mixture of equal volumes of hydrogen and chlorine in a wide-mouthed bottle, then try if the mixture will burn. Test the gas left in the vessel with blue litmus paper. Shake up a few drops of solution of nitrate of silver with the same gas.

CHLORINE AS AN OXIDIZER.

Hydrochloric acid turns blue litmus red and throws down a white precipitate with nitrate of silver.

Again mix hydrogen and chlorine and expose to bright sunlight. If they do not explode after some time repeat the tests.

What do the experiments with antimony, phosphorus and hydrogen show about the chemical activity of chlorine?

What is the conclusion from the failure to get the gas to burn in air?

3.—Chlorine as an Oxidizer.

EXPERIMENTS.

1. Take a flask full of water saturated with chlorine and fit it with a cork and tube. The outer end of the tube must be drawn to a fine point. Insert the cork so that there is not a bubble of air left in the flask. Invert the flask as in Fig. 36, and expose to direct sunlight for several days. Then place the flask on the table, remove the cork, and quickly bring a glowing splinter to the mouth of the flask. Test the water in the flask with blue litmus solution.

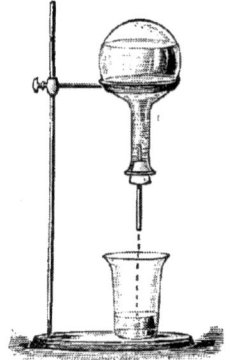

FIG. 36.

The water should give an acid re-action, and the gas should answer to the test for oxygen.

2. Pass chlorine through water that has red lead in suspension. The brown powder produced is lead dioxide, $Pb_3O_4 + 2O = 3PbO_2$.

EXPLANATION.

Chlorine is a valuable and common oxidizing agent. It produces this result by indirect action as it contains no oxygen itself. The chemical affinity between hydrogen and chlorine is sufficiently great to cause the decomposition of the water and the formation of hydrochloric acid, the oxygen being set free; and, in the nascent state, it acts energetically on any substance present that it can combine with.

4.—Bleaching by Chlorine.

EXPERIMENTS.

1. Pass a current of chlorine, or pour some chlorine water, into solutions of logwood, indigo, litmus, and writing ink.

2. Write on a piece of printed paper, with pen and ink, with an ordinary lead pencil and with colored pencil; wet the paper and drop it into chlorine for a few minutes.

Writing ink is a compound of a vegetable acid and a salt of iron (tannic acid and iron sulphate) Printer's ink is carbon ground with oil.

3. Drop into chlorine some bits of colored cotton that have been dipped in water.

Into another jar of dry gas put similar pieces of dry cotton.

What effect is produced on the colors?

How does moisture affect the result?

EXPLANATION.

Coloring matters that are capable of easy oxidation— and that generally includes those of vegetable origin—

are bleached by chlorine. This means that the compound having the distinct color has its chemical composition altered, and that the new substance does not possess the characteristic color of the original one. The chemical action involved is usually oxidation, because dry colors are scarcely affected by chlorine; but if moisture be present, and it generally is, the dehydration of the water molecules allows nascent oxygen to unite with any oxidizable substance present such as the dyes used in papers and textile fabrics.

5—Tests for Chlorine

1. Chlorine bleaches litmus.

2. It forms with nitrate of silver a curdy white precipitate, soluble in ammonia, insoluble in nitric acid.

CHAPTER XXXIII.

1—Hydrochloric Acid.

EXPERIMENTS.

1. Fit a large test-tube or a flask with a cork and a delivery tube to pass downward into a collecting jar. The materials to be used are common salt, NaCl, and sulphuric acid. Warm these gently in the flask and lead the escaping gas into a jar that has a piece of moist paper over its mouth. A bit of blue litmus paper will show when the jar is full.

Will the gas burn?

Will a candle burn in it?

Will glowing charcoal burn in it?

Is it soluble?

Pass a little of it into a bottle wet on the inside with ammonia solution.

Write an equation to express the chemical action that goes on.

Lower a little hot sodium on a chalk cup into a jar of the gas, closing the mouth of the jar with a moist card at the same time.

Is hydrogen set free in the jar?

What is the taste of the solid left on the chalk?

Common salt is NaCl. Write the equation for the chemical action.

If the gas were passed into sodium hydrate until the latter became neutral, then the liquid evaporated, what would be left?

EXPLANATION.

Hydrochloric acid is a gas that fumes strongly in the air, and is readily soluble in water. The liquid commonly called hydrochloric acid is a solution of this gas. Commercially the acid is obtained as a bye-product in alkali works, where it is produced when sodium chloride is treated with sulphuric acid as a step in the preparation of sodium carbonate. The solution of the acid is of varying strength, but about 33% by weight is the strongest solution that is permanent. Commercial acid contains about 20% of the gas.

2—Aqua Regia.

A mixture of three volumes of hydrochloric acid and one volume of nitric acid is called aqua regia.

EXPERIMENTS.

1. Place a little piece of gold leaf in chlorine water and let it stand for some time. Try what effect dry chlorine gas has on the gold leaf.

2. Place a few fragments of gold leaf in a test-tube and pour upon them a little hydrochloric acid. Warm slightly. After a minute or two add a few drops of nitric acid.

EXPLANATION.

The solvent action of *aqua regia* is due to chlorine which is freed by the action of the two acids on each other, thus:

$$HNO_3 + 3HCl = 2H_2O + NOCl + 2Cl.$$

(NOCl is chloronitrous gas, or nitrosyl chloride.) The chlorine readily attacks the gold or platinum to form the chloride which is readily soluble.

3—Composition of Hydrochloric Acid

EXPERIMENTS.

1. Take a bent tube like that in Fig. 37 Partly fill the tube, as indicated with hydrochloric acid, and insert in the ends the terminals from a battery. These terminals should be carbon. After the current has been passing for a few minutes, bring a lighted match to that end of the tube connected with the zinc of the battery. Moisten a piece of colored calico and place it over the other end of the tube. Color the acid with litmus solution.

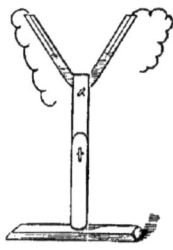

FIG. 37.

2. Pass about 25 cc. of hydrochloric acid gas into a eudiometer over mercury, then introduce sodium amalgam until the gas ceases to contract in volume; test the gas that remains, by passing in a little oxygen and igniting the mixture.

What gases compose hydrochloric acid?

What is the action of sodium on the acid?

The following simple method of determining the composition of hydrochloric acid gas is described in Reynold's *Chemistry*, Part II, page 69:—

Open the stopcock, Fig. 38, and pass a current of hydrochloric acid gas through the U-tube for some time, then quickly close the stopcock and pour mercury enough into the U-tube to close the bend and half fill the open arm. Open the stopcock slightly and allow gas to escape until the mercury stands at nearly the same height in both arms. Mark the height of the mercury in the closed arm. Next drop into the open arm some sodium amalgam and fill to the top with mercury; close the open end with the thumb, and pass the gas backward and forward a number of times through the mercury by tilting the tube, so that the amalgam will pass into the arm containing the gas. Finally hold the tube erect, raise the thumb and allow air to enter the open arm. Pour in or remove mercury until it is at the same height in both arms. The gas in the closed arm should now occupy half the volume that it did at first. Tilt the tube so that the mercury will press on the gas in the closed arm, cautiously open the stopcock and hold the nozzle to a flame.

This demonstrates that hydrochloric acid contains half its own volume of hydrogen, hence every *two* molecules of the gas contain one molecule of hydrogen; and as the density of the acid is 18·25, the molecular weight is 36·5. So that one atom of hydrogen and one atom of chlorine are combined in a molecule of the gas.

4—Tests for Hydrochloric Acid.

(1) Hydrochloric acid turns blue litmus red.

(2) It forms a white precipitate with nitrate of silver soluble in ammonia, insoluble in nitric acid.

5.—Questions and Exercises

1. Half fill a test tube with hydrogen over water, then fill it up with chlorine, and let it stand over water for a few hours in diffused light. Test, with litmus paper, and with nitrate of silver solution, the water that passes into the tube.

2. Treat the residue from preparing oxygen from manganese dioxide and chlorate of potash with sulphuric acid, and observe what gas is evolved. How is this accounted for? What is the residue chemically?

3. If chlorine bleaches by oxidation, and you wish to remove ink-stains from a handkerchief, why not plunge it into a jar of oxygen rather than into one of chlorine?

4. Lower a piece of glowing charcoal gradually into a jar of chlorine; from the negative result of this experiment, explain the formation of the black smoke which escapes from the candle when burning in chlorine.

5. Try if other chlorides may be substituted for common salt in the preparation of chlorine and hydrochloric acid.

6. The oxidizing power of chlorine may be shown in the following way.—

There are three oxides of lead, the protoxide, PbO, a buff or yellow powder, the red oxide, Pb_3O_4, a scarlet powder, and the peroxide, PbO_2, a dark brown powder. They are all insoluble in water. If a little of the protoxide and of the red oxide be shaken up separately with water in test-tubes, and chlorine be then passed through the mixtures until the water is saturated, and the whole allowed to stand for some hours, the yellow and red powders will both be changed to brown, thus showing the change to the peroxide. This change may be hastened by using solution of potassic or sodic hydrate instead of water as the liquid with which the powder is mixed. Why?

7. Wet a piece of blotting paper with oil of turpentine, $C_{10}H_{16}$, and then place it in a jar of chlorine. Use fresh and perfectly fluid turpentine.

CHAPTER XXXIV.

1.—Bleaching Powder.

Bleaching powder, or chloride of lime, is an important article of commerce which is extensively used in bleaching the coarser kinds of cotton and linen goods. Its manufacture is illustrated in the following experiments.

EXPERIMENTS.

1. Cover the inside of a bell jar with slaked lime, and then pass chlorine into it for some time. The chemical changes which take place may be thus represented:—

$$2Cl_2 + \underbrace{2Ca(HO)_2}_{\text{Slaked lime}} = 2H_2O + \underbrace{CaCl_2}_{\text{Calcium chloride}} + \underbrace{Ca(ClO)_2}_{\text{Calcium hypochlorite.}}$$

It is this mixture of calcium chloride and calcium hypochlorite which forms the most important ingredients of what is commonly known as "bleaching powder." It is the chlorinated lime, or chloride of lime, of the drug store; and is prepared by saturating slaked lime spread on shelves with chlorine gas.

Make a thin paste of bleaching powder in water. Immerse in the solution thus prepared a piece of printed calico. After a few minutes remove the calico and immerse it in a *very* dilute solution of sulphuric acid.

Bleaching powder, when acted on by an acid, yields chlorine slowly, thus with sulphuric acid the re-action is:

$$Ca(ClO)_2 + CaCl_2 + 2H_2SO_4 = 2CaSO_4 + 2H_2O + 2Cl_2.$$

This is the result of three separate actions.

(1) $Ca(ClO)_2 + H_2SO_4 = CaSO_4 + 2HClO$ (hypochlorous acid)

(2) $CaCl_2 + H_2SO_4 = CaSO_4 + 2HCl.$

(3) $\qquad HCl + HClO = H_2O + 2Cl.$

EXPLANATION.

In some manufacturing operations, especially those connected with the preparation of linen, cotton and paper goods, bleaching is an essential part of the work. A convenient method of securing this result is to immerse the material from which the color is to be removed in a bath containing a thin paste of bleaching powder, then subjecting it to the action of weak acid. The carbonic acid of the atmosphere is sufficient to bring about the chemical action, though slowly.

2.—Chlorine and the Alkaline Hydrates.

When chlorine is passed into a *cold*, dilute solution of potassium hydrate, a chemical action according to the following equation occurs —

$$2KOH + Cl_2 = KCl + KClO + H_2O$$

Potassic chloride, potassic hypochlorite and water are produced

If the solution of the hydrate were *hot* and concentrated a different combination would occur, thus:—

$$6KHO + 3Cl_2 = 5KCl + KClO_3 + 3H_2O.$$

The re-action expressed above really occurs in two steps, thus:—

$$6KHO + 3Cl_2 = 3KCl + 3KClO + 3H_2O$$
$$\text{and} \quad 3KClO = 2KCl + KClO_3.$$

The alkaline hypochlorites, in presence of hydroxides, are easily changed by heat into the chloride and chlorate.

3.—Potassium Chlorate.

EXPERIMENTS.

1. Boil a strong solution of caustic potash in a test-tube and pass into it a current of chlorine for half an hour. Evaporate the solution to a small quantity and then allow it to cool slowly. Both potassic chloride KCl, and potassic chlorate $KClO_3$, will be formed in the solution. The latter being the least soluble crystallizes out *first*. The liquid that remains contains the potassic chloride in solution. Pour off this liquid. To purify the crystals re-dissolve them in a little hot water and allow them to re-form.

All the oxygen compounds of chlorine are unstable, and most of them are explosive, breaking up into chlorine and oxygen. The alkaline chlorates are used for the preparation of oxygen in the laboratory, partly because of this instability, partly because of the relatively large quantity of gas set free.

2. Put a crystal of chlorate of potash about the size of a pea into a test-tube, then drop in a little sulphuric

acid and heat gently. While pouring in the acid, and while heating, hold the tube so that spurting fluid will not do injury.

The rather violent decomposition that goes on is expressed by the following equation —

$$3KClO_3 + 2H_2SO_4 = 2ClO_2 + KClO_4 + 2KHSO_4 + H_2O.$$

This is the sum of the following re-actions:—

$$2KClO_3 + 2H_2SO_4 = 2KHSO_4 + 2HClO_3 \text{ (chloric acid)}.$$

$$2HClO_3 + KClO_3 = 2ClO_2 + H_2O + KClO_4.$$

The sulphuric acid and chlorate give rise to chloric acid, which immediately breaks up into chloric peroxide, water and oxygen, the latter uniting with a molecule of the chlorate to oxidize it to perchlorate.

3. In a conical vessel, such as a graduate, place a few crystals of chlorate of potash, on these lay two or three bits of freshly-cut phosphorus, cover the whole with water to a depth of a couple of inches; then, by means of a pipette, introduce a few drops of strong sulphuric acid among the lumps of chlorate. Compare this experiment with the preceding one and explain the result. Trace the chemical actions throughout and account for the flashes of flame.

4. Powder some more of the salt with dry sugar. Place the mixture on a tin plate or piece of cardboard, and add a drop or two of sulphuric acid with a pipette.

5 Powder separately, and dry on a warm plate, some sulphur and chlorate of potash. Rub a *little* of the mixture on an iron plate with a pestle or hammer. This is dangerous, so only *small* quantities of the mixture should be made and used.

6 Dissolve a crystal of a chlorate in water, add a little indigo solution, and then a few drops of sulphuric acid Explain the cause of the change of color.

TESTS FOR A CHLORATE.—This property of yielding oxygen and leaving a *chloride* as residue distinguishes the chlorates.

4—Oxides and Acids

Oxygen forms with chlorine three known oxides and two hypothetical ones.

FORMULA	NAME	CORRESPONDING ACID
Cl_2O.	Hypochlorous anhydride	$HClO$ Hypochlorous acid
Cl_2O_3.	Chlorous anhydride	$HClO_2$ Chlorous acid.
Cl_2O_4, (ClO_2)	Chloric peroxide	No corresponding acid.
Cl_2O_5	Not eliminated	$HClO_3$ Chloric acid.
Cl_2O_7	Not eliminated	$HClO_4$ Perchloric acid.

Just as sodium nitrate, $NaNO_3$, yields nitric acid when treated with sulphuric acid, and sodium chloride, $NaCl$, yields hydrochloric acid; so potassium chlorate, $KClO_3$, yields chloric acid, $HClO_3$, and potassium hypochlorite yields hypochlorous acid, $HClO$. Thus:—

$$2NaNO_3 + H_2SO_4 = Na_2SO_4 + 2HNO_3,$$
$$2NaCl + H_2SO_4 = Na_2SO_4 + 2HCl,$$
$$2KClO_3 + H_2SO_4 = K_2SO_4 + 2HClO_3,$$
$$2KClO + H_2SO_4 = K_2SO_4 + 2HClO.$$

As chloric and hypochlorous acids, however, break up with dangerous explosions as soon as formed, the student is warned not to attempt to prepare them in this way.

5.—Uses of Chlorine and its Compounds.

Chlorine and the chlorates are useful oxidizing agents in chemical operations.

Because of its power of oxidation it is capable of altering many dyes and coloring substances to others without distinctive colors; chlorine gas and hypochlorous acid are chiefly employed in this work. Bleaching powder is the most convenient substance to use for the purpose because it can be easily applied at the place where it is needed and the decomposition that sets free the chlorine is readily brought about.

There is no more common disinfectant and deodorant than chloride of lime (bleaching powder). When treated with a little weak acid, as vinegar, chlorine and hypochlorous acid are both given off and become mixed with the air in the room, these are destructive, both of disease germs and of their breeding places.

6.—Questions and Exercises.

1. How can the chlorate of potash be converted into the chloride?

2. What physical state do the compounds formed in an explosion usually assume?

3. A chloride treated with sulphuric acid yields hydrochloric acid. Could nitric acid be substituted for sulphuric? Could hydrochloric? If a strong oxidizing agent were present when the hydrochloric acid is set free, what result would follow? If some chlorate were mixed with the chloride, what should be looked for as the re-actions go on?

4. How much chlorine by weight and volume can be obtained from 1,460 grams of hydric chloride?

5. How much chlorine can be liberated from 585 grams of common salt? What volume will it occupy at 60° F.?

6. What volume will 284 grams of chlorine occupy at 80° F ?

7. If the waste pipe of a kitchen sink were foul smelling, describe a method of deodorizing it.

8. How might chloride of lime be employed to disinfect a room?

9. Mention any advantage that results from the use of bleaching powder as a disinfectant in a room, rather than chlorine prepared from hydrochloric acid and manganese dioxide.

10. Chlorine will decompose oxide of hydrogen, H_2O; sulphide of hydrogen, H_2S, is less stable than the oxide. What result might be looked for if chlorine gas were passed into a solution of hydrogen sulphide?

11. What would be the result of passing a current of chlorine into limewater?

12. Why should chlorate of potash decompose quietly when heated alone, but violently when heated with sulphuric acid?

CHAPTER XXXV.

1.—Sulphur.

EXPERIMENTS.

1. Place some sulphur on a metal spoon, or in a chalk cup, and hold it in a flame until ignited, then withdraw it.

What color is the flame?

Smell the gas very cautiously that comes off.

Hold a bit of moist blue litmus paper where the gas will come in contact with it.

Find if the gas is soluble by lowering some burning sulphur into a bottle, and, after the bottle is full of gas, inverting it over water.

Is sulphur soluble in water?

Is it soluble in alcohol, ether, chloroform or carbon bisulphide?

2. Place sulphur to a depth of two inches in a large test-tube and heat slowly over a lamp flame until it boils. As the heating goes on, note changes in the appearance of the sulphur When it begins to boil, pour it into a vessel of cold water

What appearance had vapor of sulphur as it came off from the boiling liquid?

Compare the substance in the water with the original sulphur.

Will the brown substance burn?

What kind of a flame is produced?

Does the gas given off during combustion resemble that from common sulphur?

Is the brown substance sulphur?

What properties have been found to belong to sulphur?

EXPLANATION.

Sulphur commonly consists either of a yellow powder deposited from the vapor given off during distillation of the impure material, or of yellow sticks got by melting the powder (flowers of sulphur) and casting it in moulds. When, however, the boiling mass is poured into cold water it takes an allotrophic form quite different from the ordinary one. It is then named **plastic sulphur.**

A third modification may be obtained by melting some sulphur in a beaker, then allowing it to cool until a thin crust forms on its surface. If a couple of small holes be punched in this crust and the molten interior poured out; then, after cooling, if the surface layer be carefully lifted off, a mass of needle-shaped crystals will be found projecting from the walls

Both forms revert to yellow sulphur in time.

2.—Notes on Sulphur.

Symbol, S ; atomic weight, 32 , specific weight in the form of crystals, 2 05, (water = 1).

Sulphur, known also as brimstone, is found native in many volcanic regions, for instance, about the vents of Mount Vesuvius it occurs mixed with ashes and other impurities It is collected, carried down the mountain side, and distilled in order to free it from foreign substances; the vapor being led into cold chambers (sometimes a pit in the earth answering that purpose) where it is deposited as the yellow powder of commerce. (Flowers of sulphur.)

Sulphur occurs extensively in combination as sulphides and sulphates Some examples are iron pyrites, FeS_2, arsenical pyrite, $FeSAs$, galena PbS, and sulphides of copper, nickel and silver, sulphates of barium and calcium, as heavy spar and gypsum respectively, are valuable minerals.

CHAPTER XXXVI.

OXIDES OF SULPHUR.

There are two oxides of sulphur known—the dioxide SO_2 and the trioxide SO_3.

1—Sulphur Dioxide.

EXPERIMENTS.

1. In a flask, fitted with a cork and delivery tube, heat some copper clippings and sulphuric acid.

$$Cu + H_2SO_4 = CuSO_4 + 2H$$
$$\text{and } 2H + H_2SO_4 = 2H_2O + SO_2.$$

These equations are usually written thus:—

$$Cu + 2H_2SO_4 = CuSO_4 + 2H_2O + SO_2.$$

Collect some of the gas, test for solubility, acidity and inflammability.

Compare this gas with that obtained by burning sulphur.

2. Shake some of the gas with solutions of logwood, indigo and permanganate of potash.

3. Zinc, with cold dilute sulphuric acid, yields hydrogen. What is the result if zinc be dropped into hot, concentrated acid?

Will nascent hydrogen decompose sulphuric acid? Compare with effect on nitric acid, page 104.

4. An easy method for the preparation of sulphur dioxide is to treat some *sodium hyposulphite* $Na_2S_2O_3$ (which is chemically sodium thiosulphate) with sulphuric acid. The gas given off will not be pure dioxide.

$$Na_2S_2O_3 + H_2SO_4 = Na_2SO_4 + H_2S_2O_3$$
$$\text{and } H_2S_2O_3 = H_2O + SO_2 + S.$$

5. Shake some of the gas with water, and test the solution with barium chloride or barium nitrate solution. Let the solution stand in an open vessel for a day or two, then repeat the test.

How does the result differ from the former one?

Has the composition of the liquid changed meantime? If there is a change it may be entirely an internal one, or it may be due to absorption of air.

EXPLANATION.

A white precipitate thrown down by a soluble barium salt points to the presence of sulphuric acid or a soluble sulphate.

What chemical changes probably went on from the time SO_2 was passed into the water?

2.—Notes on Sulphur Dioxide.

Symbol, SO_2; molecular weight, 64, vapor density, 32, ($H = 1$).

Sulphur dioxide is the anhydride of sulphurous acid. When SO_2 is dissolved in water it tends strongly to combine with oxygen, hence is a powerful reducing agent. On this account it is used extensively in bleaching and disinfecting operations; but in this case the results are obtained by the chemical alteration through **deoxidation** of the coloring matters or the noxious substances that it is desired to be free from. It acts, therefore, in a way just the reverse of that in which chlorine does.

3 —Sulphur Trioxide.

Sulphur dioxide, as a gas, does not burn in air or oxygen and does not commonly undergo oxidation. In presence of nitrogen tetroxide, NO_2, the sulphur dioxide takes up an atom of oxygen to each molecule, thus: $NO_2+SO_2=NO+SO_3$. Also if sulphur dioxide and oxygen be passed over red-hot platinum sponge a union is brought about and the trioxide is formed. To secure this result a three-way tube is employed, sulphur dioxide being led in at one branch, oxygen at a second, while in the third which serves as an exit, a bit of platinum sponge is kept red-hot and as the mixed gases come in contact with the metal they combine and SO_3 passes out as a white powdery solid. This oxide is chiefly important as the anhydride of sulphuric acid.

CHAPTER XXXVII.

1.—Hydrogen and Sulphur

Sulphur and hydrogen form one compound that is of very general application in chemical operations, and is an agent extensively applied in the separation of some of the more commonly-occurring elements. This is *hydrogen sulphide, sulphuretted hydrogen* or *hydrosulphuric acid*, H_2S.

EXPERIMENTS.

1. Pour some dilute sulphuric acid on some iron sulphide (prepared by roasting a mixture of iron filings and about two-thirds as much sulphur, by weight, in a closed crucible). $FeS+H_2SO_4=FeSO_4+H_2S$.

Will the gas burn?

If so, invert a vessel over the flame, collect some of the products of combustion and test with litmus paper.

Is SO_2 formed in the burning?

Is H_2S soluble? If so, test the solution with litmus.

Prepare some test paper by boiling a little acetate of lead in water, then dipping strips of soft white paper in the solution.

Hold one of these strips in the gas.

Dip another in the solution of the gas.

Let a drop of the solution of the gas fall on a piece of clean silver. Rub the dark spot with a little strong ammonia solution.

Pass a current of chlorine into a jar filled with hydrogen sulphide. $H_2S + 2Cl = 2HCl + S$ Make a solution of H_2S, partly fill a bottle with it, cork the bottle and set it away for a month. Does it then contain hydrogen sulphide?

EXPLANATION.

The hydrogen sulphide undergoes decomposition by absorbing oxygen from the air, with which the hydrogen unites, and setting sulphur free as a grey powder.
$$H_2S + O = H_2O + S.$$

2. Make solutions of copper sulphate, iron sulphate, lead acetate, calcium chloride, potassium carbonate; add a few drops of hydrochloric acid to each, then pass hydrogen sulphide into the solutions (a strong solution of the gas will answer). Make each of the foregoing solutions alkaline with ammonia, and notice the results when hydrogen sulphide is added.

EXPLANATION.

This experiment illustrates the use of hydrogen sulphide in chemical analysis. It serves to separate the metals into groups, (1) those whose sulphides (the precipitates that appear) are thrown down in acid solutions, as lead and copper ; (2) those whose sulphides are soluble in acid solutions, but not in alkaline ones, as iron ; (3) those whose sulphides are soluble in both acid and alkaline solutions, as calcium and potassium.

2.—Notes on Hydrogen Sulphide.

Symbol, H_2S ; mol. wt, 34 ; mol vol., 2

It is a poisonous gas, soluble in water in proportion of 3 to 1 by volume, occurs frequently in natural waters of springs, and is formed largely in the decay of organic matters, particularly those of an albuminous nature, eggs, for example

Tests for the gas are (1) its odor, (2) its effect on acetate of lead solution, or paper dipped in it, and (3) its effect on silver.

CHAPTER XXXVIII.
ACIDS OF SULPHUR.

Sulphur, in union with hydrogen and oxygen, forms two well-known acids, **sulphurous** and **sulphuric**.

1.—Sulphurous Acid.

EXPERIMENTS.

1. Pass some sulphur dioxide gas slowly into water in a bottle. After some time test the water with litmus.

2. Divide the solution made in the previous experiment into two parts, with one of these fill a small bottle,

cork it tightly and set it away for a couple of **days**. Pour a few drops of the other part into a test-tube, add a little solution of barium nitrate (there should be no precipitate), then a drop or two of silver nitrate solution; set the remainder of this part away in an open beaker beside the bottle just mentioned. At the end of two or three days test each part of the liquid again. (Barium nitrate alone gives a white precipitate with sulphuric acid, but in the case of sulphurous acid this precipitate does not appear until silver nitrate is added.)

For an explanation of the change refer to the paragraph on sulphur dioxide, page 180.

2.—Sulphuric Acid.

EXPERIMENTS.

Pass the brown gas, NO_2, that comes from treating a metal with hot nitric acid into a large flask that contains a little water, at the same time pass in sulphur dioxide gas. After a few minutes test the liquid with barium chloride, or barium nitrate solution. A white precipitate indicates sulphuric acid.

EXPLANATION.

Sulphur dioxide in presence of water or steam will readily reduce nitrogen peroxide to nitric oxide, and thus become itself oxidized to sulphuric acid.

$$SO_2 + NO_2 + H_2O = H_2SO_4 + NO.$$

In either case the nitric oxide in presence of air at once changes back to the higher oxide and is ready to yield up oxygen again; thus, this gas serves simply as a medium for transferring oxygen from the air to the sulphurous acid.

3—Notes on Sulphuric Acid.

Sulphuric acid is a most important agent in many industrial operations; for instance, in the manufacture of fertilizers for soils, in alkali works, and in ore reduction processes. In England alone one million tons per year of sulphuric acid is made. Its chief employment comes from its power of replacing other acid radicals in chemical combinations.

On a large scale the acid is manufactured by passing into lead-lined chambers sulphur dioxide, nitrogen peroxide, steam and air. The sulphur dioxide is obtained by heating iron pyrites, FeS_2 in air, both the iron and the sulphur becoming oxidized, the latter passing off as SO_2. The peroxide of nitrogen, NO_2, is formed from decomposing nitrates; its function is to transfer oxygen from the air to the sulphurous acid so as to oxidize it to the *ic* acid. Leaden chambers are used for the condensation because that metal is scarcely affected by the cold acid.

4.—Vapor Density of Sulphur.

The density of a gas is one half its molecular weight (see page 144) This follows from Avogadro's law and from the relation of the hydrogen molecule to the hydrogen atom.

In the case of sulphur, it is found that near its boiling point (485°) the vapor density is 96, while at 850°, this density is 32, in round numbers. When the vapor density is 96 the molecular weight must be 192, but at the higher temperature mentioned the molecular weight will be 64. Chemical analysis leads to the belief that sulphur has an atomic weight of 32 From this it is clear that, at about 500°, the molecule of sulphur consists of 6 atoms; but at 850° and above that to 1,200°, the molecule has in it only 2 atoms. A change of temperature, therefore, modifies the molecular structure of the substance, as is indicated by the change in the vapor density This is illustrative of a molecular breaking down that is by no means uncommon. Decreased density at higher temperatures means an increased number of molecules without change of mass, therefore a smaller number of atoms in the single molecule.

5.—Questions and Exercises.

1. Hang a red rose, or other high-colored flower, in a jar of SO_2. If any change takes place in the flower, remove it and place in pure air

2 Drop a lump of white sugar into some strong sulphuric acid in an evaporating dish ; let it stand for 24 hours, then dilute largely with water, filter, wash with water, dry and examine carefully. Try if a little of the black substance will burn on mica. Heat some of it in a combustion tube and lead the gas into limewater See preparation of carbon monoxide, page 142.

Sugar is $C_{12}H_{22}O_{11}$. How is the blackening accounted for?

What remains of the sugar? Will starch $C_6H_{10}O_5$ yield similar results with the acid? What effect has sulphuric acid on wood?

3. Sulphur and sulphuric acid, heated together yield SO_2, thus:
$$S + H_2SO_4 = 2SO_2 + 2H,$$
$$2H + H_2SO_4 = 2H_2O + SO_2,$$
hence $S + 2H_2SO_4 = 3SO_2 + 2H_2O.$

Charcoal and sulphuric acid, heated together act as follows.
$C + 2H_2SO_4 = CO_2 + $ [complete this]

Manganese dioxide and sulphur, when heated, yield manganese sulphide and sulphur dioxide :—
$MnO_2 + 2S = MnS + SO_2.$

QUESTIONS AND EXERCISES.

4. What chemical action might be expected if sulphur dioxide were passed into: (*a*) a solution of hydrogen peroxide, H_2O_2; (*b*) a solution of chlorine; (*c*) a solution of ammonia?

5. Hydrogen sulphide is one of the constituents of illuminating gas that has to be removed as an impurity. Why is it objectionable since it burns freely?

6. How may the blackening of silver articles be accounted for in dwellings in which coal is burned as fuel and gas burned for lighting? How may the black stains be removed?

7. Is sulphide of silver soluble in ammonia or in nitric acid? To secure the sulphide add a few drops of silver nitrate solution to a solution of H_2S.

8. Hydrogen burns readily to its oxide, so does sulphur; what should be the result, then, of passing hydrogen sulphide over red-hot copper oxide?

9. Will other sulphides than that of iron yield sulphuretted hydrogen when treated with sulphuric acid? Try galena, for instance.

10. Describe methods by which sulphurous acid, or sulphur dioxide may be used to disinfect (1) a mouldy cellar; (2) a foul smelling waste pipe, (3) a room in which a case of infectious disease has been.

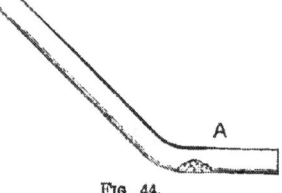

FIG. 44.

11. Bend a piece of hard glass tubing as shown in Fig. 44. Place in it at A some iron pyrites and heat strongly in a flame, holding the longer arm of the tube at about 45° with the vertical. Smell the gas that comes off.

CHAPTER XXXIX.

Calculation of Formulas.

In Chapter XXVI the calculation of empirical formulas of compounds was discussed when the percentage composition was known. At that time one important fact for the accurate determination of the molecular formulas had not been learned, viz.: that the vapor density of a substance is one-half its molecular weight. Vapor density is always taken with hydrogen as the unit. A couple of examples will be solved to show the application of this principle:—

1. A compound, on analysis yielded

$$\text{hydrogen,} \quad 2\cdot25\%,$$
$$\text{carbon,} \quad 26\cdot65\%,$$
$$\text{oxygen,} \quad 71\cdot2\%.$$

Its vapor density is 45, find its formula.

$$2\cdot25 \div 1 = 2\cdot25,$$
$$26\cdot65 \div 12 = 2\cdot25,$$
$$71\cdot2 \div 16 = 4\cdot45.$$

Neglecting what are probably errors of experiment, the elements are present in proportion of 1, 1 and 2. The formula may, therefore, be HCO_2, $H_2C_2O_4$, $H_3C_3O_6$, or generally $H_nC_nO_{2n}$. The vapor density is 45, therefore the molecular weight is 90. Now, starting with the lowest empirical formula, we find that it gives a molecular weight of 45, just half that required. We must, therefore, double the number of atoms, and write the formula $H_2C_2O_4$, (oxalic acid)

2. A hydrocarbon, when analyzed, gave hydrogen, 7·7%; carbon, 92·2%; its vapor density is 39, determine its formula.

$$7\cdot 7 \div 1 = 7\,7,$$

$$92\cdot 2 \div 12 = 7\,7.$$

Therefore the proportions of hydrogen and carbon are as 1 to 1. Hence the formula is $H_n C_n$, where n is any integer. The molecular weight of the substance is $39 \times 2 = 78$.

The molecular weight of HC is 13.

$78 \div 13 = 6$, hence formula is $C_6 H_6$, (benzine).

CHAPTER XL.

Impurities in Air and Water.

It is desirable that every one should be able to determine, approximately at least, the degree of purity of the two substances which are most necessary for our existence, in order that hurtful impurities may be removed or rejected. These substances are the air we breathe and the water we use for drinking and for domestic purposes.

1 — Air.

The atmosphere is a mixture of a number of gaseous substances some of which are quite variable in quantity; but it is generally considered that a mixture of oxygen and nitrogen in the proportion of 21% by volume of the former to 79% of the latter shall be taken as pure air. The chief gases mixed with these are aqueous vapor, carbon dioxide, and traces of ammonia with minute portions of argon, helium, neon, xenon and krypton

When it is necessary to test the purity of air for breathing in such places as school rooms, dwellings and lecture halls, the quantity of carbonic acid gas per thousand volumes is generally taken as the test of purity. This is not an absolute test, for there may be, and indeed generally are, other objectionable and deleterious products of respiration present, but as they always accompany the carbon dioxide the latter is used as the basis of the measurement. There are about 4 parts of carbon dioxide to 10,000 of air in the atmosphere. When the proportion rises above 10 in 10,000, on account of impurities due to respiration, the air becomes very objectionable for breathing. Exhaled air contains about 4% of carbon dioxide; and an adult person breathes out about fifteen cubic feet of this gas per day.

When twenty volumes of air shaken with one volume of saturated limewater shows a trace of whitening that air is becoming unfit for respiration.

2.—Water.

Pure water is both scarce and difficult to prepare. Probably the purest natural water is that which has recently fallen as rain, away from the neighborhood of towns and factories. It is then much in the condition of the water prepared by distillation. Water which has lain in contact with the earth for some time is sure to become impregnated with mineral salts and decaying matters of various kinds.

Natural waters are classified as *hard* and *soft*.

Water that contains magnesium, and calcium salts, and that curdles soap, is said to be *hard;* water that does not contain these salts is *soft.* Hardness is usually considered as being of two kinds, viz., *temporary* and *permanent.* The former is due to the presence of calcic and magnesic carbonates, which may be precipitated by boiling; the latter to the presence of salts of calcium and magnesium other than the carbonates, such as sulphates, nitrates or chlorides which cannot be thus precipitated.

Water that is temporarily hard may be softened by boiling, because the carbonates are held in solution by the carbonic acid dissolved in the water or the bicarbonate is itself soluble. Boiling expels the carbon dioxide or decomposes the bicarbonate and the carbonate is precipitated.

Water that is permanently hard may be frequently softened by the use of washing soda—neutral sodium carbonate, Na_2CO_3. (See p. 135.)

The two following equations represent the re-action of washing soda on salts in two kinds of hard water —

$$H_2Ca(CO_3)_2 + Na_2CO_3 = CaCO_3 + 2NaHCO_3$$
$$CaSO_4 + Na_2CO_3 = Na_2SO_4 + CaCO_3.$$

Water suitable for drinking is described as **potable.** That which comes from springs generally contains mineral salts, such as the carbonate of calcium or other substances through which the water has trickled, in solution. These salts are not necessarily objectionable—indeed the flat taste of rain water and of distilled water is due to the absence of them, and to the lack of aeration.

Organic matters, however, when held in solution, frequently render water dangerous to use. One test for such impurities depends on the decolorization of permanganate of potash by them.

Place the water to be tested in a flask, and add to it, first, a few drops of sulphuric acid, and then enough of a solution of permanganate of potash to give to the whole a purple tint. Set to one side for three or four hours in a warm place, and if the solution loses its color, organic impurities are present. Water that will thus decolorize permanganate of potash is in all probability unfit for drinking. If it is necessary to use such water, it should first be boiled for at least half an hour.

CHAPTER XLI.

1—Molecules of Elements Usually Consist of More Than One Atom

The only perfectly reliable means which we possess for ascertaining the molecular weight of a compound is the determination of its *vapor density*.

It follows from Avogadro's law that the weights of individual molecules of different gases is proportional to the weights of equal volumes of these gases. All we have to do then, in order to find the relative weights of molecules of different gases, is to weigh equal volumes of them under like conditions of temperature and pressure, and the numbers thus obtained will represent the relative weights of a single molecule of each gas. Manifestly, any gas might be taken as a standard with which to compare the weights of all other gaseous substances; but, for many reasons, it has been found preferable to take hydrogen as the unit of comparison.

The following facts have been established by actual weighing:—

1 litre of oxygen weighs . . . . . 1·429 gram.
1 " nitrogen " . . 1·2553 "
1 " chlorine " . . . . 3·167 "
1 " hydrochloric acid gas weighs 1·6283 "
1 " hydrogen weighs . . . . 0·896 "

(The weight of hydrogen is obtained by calculation from the two preceding data, because it is exceedingly difficult to weigh a litre of hydrogen accurately, on account of its lightness.)

Now, using hydrogen as the standard of comparison, it follows from the above data that oxygen is nearly sixteen times heavier than hydrogen, nitrogen, nearly fourteen times heavier, and chlorine, 35·34 times heavier. Hence, these figures represent the number of times that a molecule of each of these elements is heavier than a molecule of hydrogen. It follows, further, that if we know the actual number of atoms composing each of these molecules, we should be able to calculate their atomic weights. If there are the same number of atoms (say two) in each molecule of these elements, the above figures will also represent their atomic weights, one atom of hydrogen being taken as the standard. Modern investigation has established that the portion of matter taking part in chemical actions is not the ultimate unit of matter, but that this portion is itself an aggregation of varying complexity. This need not interfere with the convention usually adopted in elementary chemistry, that the smallest portion of an element entering into union with other elements is the chemical unit which we shall still call an *atom*

2.—The Molecule of Oxygen Consists of at Least Two Atoms

Two volumes of hydrogen and one volume of oxygen unite to form two volumes of steam

From this it follows that two molecules of hydrogen and one molecule of oxygen unite to form two molecules of water. In one molecule of water there must be one molecule of hydrogen and half a molecule of oxygen, therefore this half molecule must consist of at least one atom.

3—The Hydrogen Molecule Consists of Two Atoms at Least

We have seen in Chap XXXIII, page 168, that two volumes of hydrochloric acid gas may be broken into one volume of hydrogen and one volume of chlorine. One volume of the acid may, therefore, be divided into half a volume of hydrogen and half a volume of chlorine. Then one molecule of the acid consists of half a molecule of each constituent, and this half molecule must be at least one atom ; hence, the molecule of hydrogen has in it two atoms at least

Since this substance is the standard for vapor density comparison, we have to rely on other considerations for the proof that the molecule consists of only two atoms. Some of these are —In compounds of hydrogen with monad elements the combinations and decompositions take place each at one stage; never is part of the hydrogen freed from the other element, and then by changed or intensified treatment, the other part liberated. On the other hand, when hydrogen unites with a diad element, half of it may frequently be displaced at once, and the other half at another time. Thus:—

$$H_2O + Na = NaHO + H$$
and $$NaHO + Na = Na_2O + H.$$

With monads such displacements are manifestly impossible.

When decomposition of such compounds (hydrogen with monad elements) occurs, the hydrogen always occupies one-half the space of the original gas; hence, from two molecules of the compound, one molecule of hydrogen is set free. The same conclusion is arrived at from the consideration that in equal volumes of hydrogen and hydrochloric acid gas, the weight of hydrogen in the latter, when freed, is just half that of the former; hence, in equal volumes of hydrogen and hydrochloric acid, the number of molecules being equal, the number of hydrogen molecules formed from the latter gas equals half that existing in the former. Since in chemical decompositions the quantity of hydrogen freed from combination with monad elements is the unit of volume, of which that liberated from other combinations is always an integral multiple, it is reasonable to conclude that we have here the smallest subdivisions of the hydrogen molecule which are chemically active, *i.e.*, half molecules or atoms.

4.—Nitrogen Molecules.

When nitrous oxide was decomposed by burning potassium (see page 97), a volume of nitrogen equal to that of the original gas remained. When nitric oxide was similarly treated the nitrogen remaining was half that of the gas taken. Now it will be evident that equal volumes of the two oxides contain equal numbers of molecules, and that every molecule of the nitrous oxide contains nitrogen sufficient to form one molecule of that gas, while in the case of the nitric oxide each molecule contains only half a molecule of nitrogen, hence the molecule of nitrogen is divisible into two equal parts, hence, contains at least two atoms.

5.—Chlorine Molecules.

We have learned that the hydrogen molecule has in it two atoms; also one volume of hydrogen unites with one volume of chlorine to form two volumes of hydrochloric acid. The analysis of the latter shows that it is composed of equal parts, by volume, of hydrogen and chlorine; then, since one volume of the gas is made up of half a volume of hydrogen and half a volume of chlorine, it follows that one molecule of it is composed of half a molecule of hydrogen and half a molecule of chlorine; hence, the chlorine molecule is divisible into two equal parts, or at least into two atoms.

6.—Other Elements.

Starting with the compounds marsh gas and sulphur dioxide, the conclusion follows that sulphur and carbon molecules are also divisible into at least two equal parts or atoms.

The student must not understand, however, that this is a proof that there are only two atoms in the molecules of these substances. While that is probably the case with most elements, it has already been shown that for sulphur there are six atoms in the molecule at certain temperatures. Phosphorus and arsenic have each a four-atom molecule, while ozone has three, and mercury one.

In the case of compounds, it follows directly from the atomic theory that the molecule must consist of a group of atoms,—one at least from each constituent.

CHAPTER XLII

THEORY OF DISSOCIATION IN SOLUTION.

1.—Definition.

The term **dissociation** in chemistry is applied to the decomposition of a compound under such conditions that the components will re-unite if the influences that caused the decomposition be removed. For instance, ammonium chloride will break up into ammonia gas and hydrochloric acid when heated; but, if the heat be stopped, these substances will re-combine to form the original salt again. Similarly, water, at a very high temperature, is separated into oxygen and hydrogen; but, if the temperature be lowered, water is again formed.

2.—Composition of Acids, Bases, and Salts.

Acids invariably consist of hydrogen in union, either with another element or a radical. The molecule may contain either one or more than one atom of hydrogen that is not part of the radical; the number of such atoms determines the **basicity** of the acid.

Bases are composed of a metal in union with hydroxyl. Each molecule consists of an atom of the metal combined with one or more of the radicals, depending on the valency of the metal.

Salts are formed by the metal of the base going into union with the non-hydrogen part of the acid. The hydrogen of the acid combines with the hydroxyl of the base to produce water.

3 —Ionization.

It has long been known that solutions of acids, bases and salts will conduct an electric current, while solutions of other substances, as sugar, glycerine, alcohol, will not. Further, in those cases in which the solution forms part of an electric circuit there is an actual transferrence of matter from some parts of the liquid mass to others. An experiment will make this clear. Some solution of. copper sulphate, $CuSO_4$, is put into the apparatus for electrolytic decomposition of water and the current passed through it. The liquid gradually loses its color, and the electrode connected with the zinc pole of the battery becomes coated with copper in a smooth hard layer. If the fluid were tested for acidity at the beginning of the operation and after it had become decolorized, that portion surrounding the electrode connected with the carbon pole of the battery would be found to have become distinctly more acid. The metal has, therefore, been transferred from all parts of the liquid to the negative electrode, while acid has gathered at the positive one. This passing of portions of the dissolved substance toward the electrodes is generally described as **the movement of the ions,** (ion meaning traveller)

It is believed that the salt molecule, in such cases, becomes decomposed, the metallic part separating from the acid and moving in one direction while the acid radical goes in the other one. Thus, there are two streams flowing in opposite directions, one made up of atoms of the metal, the other of the acid portions of the molecules, each under the influence of some force that sends the processions toward their respective goals.

4—Interaction of Salts.

It is well known that solutions of two salts will often act chemically on each other when brought together; in fact, every case of double displacement is an example of it. If the resulting salts are also soluble, the re-action does not go on to completion, but when certain portions of the original salts have interchanged parts the operation ceases. As an instance, if potassium nitrate and sodium chloride be mixed the result cannot be at all distinguished from that obtained by mixing potassium chloride and sodium nitrate. Indeed, all four salts exist in both solutions and in exactly the same proportions. When a certain stage of concentration is reached the action ceases. The salts are then said to be in equilibrium in the solution; and, if this balance is disturbed, the chemical action begins again, going either in the same direction as the former one or the reverse depending on which tends to restore the destroyed equilibrium. Such actions are described as **reversible.**

If by any process, as by precipitation or volatilization, one of the substances be removed from the solution as fast as formed, this would cause a constant disturbance of equilibrium with a consequently continuous action until the interacting salts disappear.

5.—Theory.

The explanation of these phenomena is based on a theory advanced by Arrhenius, a Swedish chemist. "Salts do not exist, as such in aqueous solution, but are dissociated more or less completely into their constituents or ions." This means in brief that when a salt goes into dilute solution, some of its molecules cease to exist as salt and become separated into basic and acidic ions, thus sodium chloride in solution has a certain proportion of its molecules divided into Na and Cl ions; similarly ammonium nitrate becomes to some extent dissociated into NH_4 and NO_3 ions. If for any reason some of these free ions be removed from solution other molecules become ionized until the balance is restored between the ionized and non-ionized portions of the salt.

When ions of two salts are in the same solution they tend to form combinations so as to establish an equilibrium between the number of free ions and the molecules arising from the new unions. If this equilibrium, when established, be disturbed in any way chemical action will be set up in that way which tends to restore the balance.

6—Electrolytic Dissociation.

The migration of the ions, when the salt solution is part of an electric circuit, is accounted for by the theory that the parts of the dissociated molecules carry electric charges.

A fundamental experiment in static electricity shows that bodies charged with opposite kinds of electricity attract each other, while those charged with the same kind repel each other. If the basic ions carry positive charges and the acid radicals are negatively charged, the former would tend to move toward the negative pole immersed in the solution, while the latter would be drawn in the opposite direction. This is actually what happens. The salt molecules, therefore, seem to be dissociated not into a metallic atom or atoms and an acid radical, but into these plus a charge of positive electricity on the former and a negative one on the latter. When these ions reach the poles electrified oppositely to themselves they give up their charges and take the properties of metal and acid radical.

As an example, potassium chloride, in solution, is partly dissociated and the molecules thus separated are represented, not by KCl, nor by $K+Cl$, but by $\overset{+}{K}+\overset{-}{Cl}$. Similarly sodium nitrate is $\overset{+}{Na}+\overset{-}{NO_3}$.

7.—Valency and Electric Charges of Ions.

It is probable that those properties of matter generally referred to as chemical affinity and valency are in some way dependent upon the quantity of electricity carried by the ions. In dissociated molecules, HCl for example, if the charge of the hydrogen ion be taken as the positive unit, that of the Cl will be the negative one; and, in all cases of dissociation, the actual quantities of positive and negative electricity must be equal. If the sign, +, above a symbol, stands for unit charge of positive electricity, and the sign, -, for the negative unit, the following formulas are typical of dissociated products —

$$H_2\overset{\prime\;\prime\prime}{O} \text{ becomes } \overset{+}{H} + \overset{-}{OH}; \; \overset{\prime\;\;\;\prime\prime}{H_2SO_4} = \overset{+}{H} + \overset{+}{H} + \overset{-,-}{SO_4}.$$

$$\overset{\prime\prime\;\;\prime}{ZnCl_2} = \overset{+,+}{Zn} + \overset{-}{Cl} + \overset{-}{Cl}; \; \overset{\prime\prime\;\;\;\prime}{Fe(OH)_2} = \overset{+,+}{Fe} + \overset{-}{OH} + \overset{-}{OH}.$$

$$\overset{\prime\prime\prime\;\;\;\prime}{Fe(NO_3)_3} = \overset{+,+,+}{Fe} + \overset{-}{NO_3} + \overset{-}{NO_3} + \overset{-}{NO_3}.$$

This does not, in any way, explain either what valency is, or why it is variable, but it does seem to point to electricity being an essential part of that which we popularly designate *matter*. Neither does it follow that ions possess the properties which distinguish the kind of matter to which they belong. Thus hydrogen and chlorine assume their distinctive characteristics only when in the molecular condition, H_2 and Cl_2, not when they are in that state represented by the symbols $\overset{+}{H}$, $\overset{-}{Cl}$.

8. — Strong and Weak Acids.

In the case of strong acids a large proportion of the molecules become dissociated in dilute solutions, while with weak acids the equilibrium already spoken of between the ionized and non-ionized molecules is established when a comparatively small number of them have become separated into basic and acid portions.

Water itself is slightly ionized into $H + OH$. It is thus, chemically, hydroxide of hydrogen; and is related to the acids by setting free a hydrogen ion from the molecule, and to the bases by separating a hydroxyl radical. The separation of the water molecule is termed **hydrolysis or hydrolytic dissociation.**

CHAPTER XLIII.

Historical.—The Beginnings of Chemistry.

While yet the phlogiston theory (page 2) held sway, knowledge was accumulating and speculations were taking form which finally led to its replacement by the science of chemistry.

Dr. Black, of Edinburgh, demonstrated that the heating of substances such as lead and mercury in air caused a change of weight, hence that there was an action involving addition or subtraction of matter, not of a principle or property. In 1774, Priestley separated oxygen as a gas, and discovered its property of supporting combustion, while almost at the same time Scheele, a Swede, announced that this gas was one of the constituents of the atmosphere. Hitherto, it had been explained that the gas given off when a metal is treated with an acid was the combustible part of the metal, but it was soon found that the gas had a different origin; and Cavendish, in 1781, demonstrated that it was one of the constituents of water, and he determined the proportions in which it combines with oxygen. Proust next discovered that the portions of elements taking part in chemical union or decomposition are definite by weight. Dalton, working at a similar problem, formulated in 1804 the theory which is the basis of modern chemistry, viz., that elements combine with one another in integral multiples of certain unit weights, now called atomic; hence that definite portions of these elements, named atoms, take part in chemical actions. Dalton was led to this conclusion by his discovery that if an element, such as oxygen, forms various combinations with another, such as carbon, the portions of the former by weight which enter into union with a unit weight of the latter are integral (simple) multiples of that which forms the lowest combination. He, therefore, argued that elements exist in portions or masses of definite weight, that for the same element these do not vary, but for different elements they are unlike ; and that when chemical action goes on these masses take part in it as wholes, a portion of an atom never having independent existence.

This was the origin of chemical science, and it was based on the principles enunciated in the statements that (1) chemical action involves matter, not mere properties, (2) that it takes place among definite portions of matter by weight, (3) that all chemical actions into which any substance enters involve portions of that substance that are simple multiples of the least portion taking part in any such action. From this time on chemistry ceased to be mere random experimentation and theorizing, and development took place in accordance with recognized laws and hypotheses.

APPENDIX.

I.

Laws of Chemical Combination.

1.—Law of Definite Proportions.

In any group of substances undergoing chemical change, the quantities (masses) taking part in the action, both as constituents and product, bear a simple fixed ratio to each other, which remains constant for any particular action or its reverse.

2.—Law of Multiple Proportions.

If two substances combine in different proportions to form distinctly different products, and if a fixed mass of one of the substances be taken, then the proportions in which the other substance combines with it are simple integral multiples of the smallest portion (mass) of that constituent entering into any of the compounds.

3—Law of Reciprocal Proportions (Equivalent Proportions).

The masses of the two substances, X and Y, that combine respectively with a unit mass of a third substance, M, are either the proportions, or when multiplied by simple, integral numbers, become the proportions, in which X and Y combine with each other, or with any other substance.

4.—Law of Conservation of Mass.

In any chemical action the sum of the masses (portions taking part in the action) of the constituents is equal to the total mass of the products.

5.—Law of Gas Volumes.

If a group of substances remain gaseous throughout a chemical action in which they take part, the volume of the constituents and that of the products are either equal, or the one is a simple, integral multiple of the other; and this relation of volumes is the same as that expressed in the molecular re-arrangements that constitute the chemical action. (See page 75.)

II.
List of Elements.

Name.	Symbol.	Atomic Weight	Name.	Symbol.	Atomic Weight
Aluminium	Al	27	Gallium	Ga	70
Antimony	Sb	119	Germanium	Ge	72
Argon	A	39·6?	Glucinum (Beryllium)	Gl	9
Arsenic	As	75	Gold	Au	197
Barium	Ba	137	Helium	He	3·9?
Bismuth	Bi	208	Hydrogen	H	1
Boron	B	11	Indium	In	114
Bromine	Br	79	Iodine	I	126
Cadmium	Cd	112	Iron	Fe	56
Cæsium	Cs	132·9	Krypton	Kr	81
Calcium	Ca	40	Lanthanum	La	138·5
Carbon	C	12	Lead	Pb	207
Cerium	Ce	140	Lithium	Li	7
Chlorine	Cl	35·5	Magnesium	Mg	24
Chromium	Cr	52	Manganese	Mn	55
Cobalt	Co	59	Mercury	Hg	200
Columbian (Niobian)	Cb	94	Molybdenum	Mo	96
Copper	Cu	63·5	Neodymium	Nd	143·5
Erbium	Er	166	Neon	Ne	19?
Fluorin	F	19	Nickel	Ni	58·7
Gadolinium	Gd	156			

List of Elements—*(Continued)*.

Name.	Symbol.	Atomic Weight	Name.	Symbol.	Atomic Weight
Nitrogen	N	14	Strontium	Sr	87·5
Osmium	Os	190·8	Sulphur	S	32
Oxygen	O	16	Tantalum	Ta	183
Palladium	Pd	106·5	Tellurium	Te	127·5
Phosphorus	P	31	Terbium	Tb	160
Platinum	Pt	195	Thallium	Tl	204
Potassium	K	39·1	Thorium	Th	230
Praseodymium	Pr	140·5	Thulium	Tu	170 ?
Radium	Ra	225	Tin	Sn	119
Rhodium	Rh	103	Titanium	Ti	48
Rubidium	Rb	85·4	Tungsten (Wolfram)	W	184
Ruthenium	Ru	101.7	Uranium	U	239
Samarium	Sm	150 ?	Vanadium	V	51·4
Scandium	Sc	44	Xenon		128 ?
Selenium	Se	79·2	Ytterbium	Yt	173
Silicon	Si	28·4	Yttrium	Y	89
Silver	Ag	107	Zinc	Zn	65
Sodium	Na	23	Zirconium	Zr	90·5

III.

Values (Approximate) of Metric Units of Weight, Length, and Volume in English Measures; and of English Units in Metric Measures.

Metric Weights.

1 gram .... = 15·4 grains.
1 centigram = 3·5 ozs., avoir.
1 kilogram = 2·2 lbs., avoir.

Metric Volumes.

1 cc. = ·064 cubic in.
1 litre = ·88 quart.

Metric Lengths.

1 mm. ..... = ·04 = $\frac{1}{25}$ in.
10 mm. (1 cm.) = $\frac{2}{5}$ in.
25 mm. ...... = 1 in.
1 metre ..... = 39·4 in.
1 kilometre.. = ·621 mile = 200 rods.

English Weights.

1 oz., avoir. = 28·5 grams.
1 lb., avoir. = 454· grams.

English Volumes.

1 fluid dram	=	3·55 cc.
1 fluid ounce	=	28·4 cc.
1 pint	=	576 cc.
1 quart	=	1150 cc.
1 cubic inch	=	16·4 cc.
1 cubic foot	=	28370 cc.
	=	28·4 litres.

English Lengths.

1 inch .... = 2·5 cm.
1 foot .... = 30 cm.
1 yard .... = ·914 m.
1 mile .... = 1·609 km.

Questions and Exercises.

1. On what grounds are hydrogen and oxygen considered to be chemical elements, and water to be a compound of these two elements?

2. Classify the changes, as physical or chemical, which occur in the following cases :—(1) sugar is dropped into water ; (2) sugar is placed on a red-hot iron plate ; (3) water is dropped on common salt ; (4) sulphuric acid is dropped on common salt ; (5) a piece of charcoal is held in a gas flame ; (6) a piece of ice is held in a gas flame , (7) some potassium is placed in water.

3. (a) Describe experiments to show that one cc of hydrogen gas and one cc. of chlorine gas are found in two cc. of hydrochloric acid gas, and one cc of oxygen gas and two cc. of hydrogen gas in two cc. of water gas.

(b) Draw the inference from the above experiments that the ratio of the weight of two cc. of each of these compound gases to the weight of one cc of hydrogen is twice the specific gravity of the compound gases compared to hydrogen.

4. Discuss the question as to the distinction between a combustible substance and a supporter of combustion. Illustrate by equations the chemical re-actions which occur in the combustion of

      (a) Hydrogen in chlorine.

      (b) Oxygen in marsh gas.

      (c) Carbon monoxide in oxygen.

      (d) Sodium in hydrochloric acid gas.

      (e) Hydrogen sulphide in oxygen.

5. Describe experiments to show that oxygen and hydrogen in the nascent condition are more active chemically than ordinary oxygen and hydrogen.

6 Some white sugar dropped into water will disappear, and, after evaporation a white solid will remain. Some zinc dropped into dilute sulphuric acid will disappear, and, after evaporation a white solid will remain. Compare the two actions.

7. A person undertook to fumigate a pantry with sulphur dioxide, but the wood became so impregnated with the gas that food was damaged by acid when put on the shelves How might this objection be removed?

8. Explain (1) the blackening of silver articles exposed to escaping furnace gas; (2) why metals that are not affected by strong acids will dissolve in chlorine water; (3) how NO is formed when nitric acid acts on copper, (4) how SO_2 is produced when sulphuric acid acts on copper; (5) why chlorine bleaches litmus.

9. Explain the meaning assigned by chemists to the following terms :—(a) Oxidizing agents, (b) reducing agents; write equations showing instances of oxidation, (c) by oxygen gas, (d) by chlorine water, (e) by nitric acid, of reduction (f) by heat, (g) by charcoal, (h) by nascent hydrogen.

10. Describe the physical changes and illustrate by equations the chemical changes which occur when each of the following substances is heated in a test-tube —(a) ammonium nitrate, (b) potassium nitrate, (c) lead nitrate, (d) calcium carbonate, (e) ammonium chloride.

11. How would you prove the presence of

(a) hydrogen and sulphur in hydrogen sulphide,

(b) carbon in carbon dioxide,

(c) nitrogen in ammonia?

12 Give one illustration in each case showing the relations of electricity, heat, and light, as a cause, and an effect of chemical action.

13. Explain, using equations, the re-actions that occur when

(a) Carbon dioxide is passed over red-hot charcoal.

(b) Dry hydrogen is passed over red-hot copper oxide.

14. Compare the action of hot sulphuric acid on copper with that of strong nitric acid on copper. Give equations.

15. Describe as fully as you can, the phenomena of a solution of a salt in water.

16. A test-tube is known to contain distilled water, or a solution of one of the following :—ammonia gas, potassium hydrate, potassium chloride, nitric acid. How would you determine most simply which the test-tube contains?

17. Explain, by means of equations, how each of the following substances bleaches —

 (*a*) Chlorine in the air.
 (*b*) Chlorine in a solution of water.
 (*c*) Sulphur dioxide gas

18. Four volumes of methane are mixed with six volumes of oxygen and the mixture exploded. Find the volume of the gas in the vessel and state its composition (1) at a temperature of 120°, (2) after the products of combustion have stood in a room at 20° c. for some time

19. Make a strong solution of ammonic chloride in a beaker, test the solution with litmus. Then hang a piece of litmus paper just above the liquid, but not touching it, place another piece in the solution, and boil the contents of the beaker for half an hour. State what will occur, and explain the chemical action.

20. Nitric acid may be prepared by heating sodic nitrate with sulphuric acid. When the other substance formed is acid sulphate of sodium, find in what proportions the substances must be taken that none of either may be left. What is acid sulphate of sodium? When is such a salt possible? Write the equation for the other re-action possible between the substances

21. A piece of sodium was completely converted into chloride by uniting with 200 cc. of Cl. at the standard temperature and pressure. What was the weight of the sodium?

If the 200 cc had been hydrochloric acid gas what volume of hydrogen would have remained?

22. How many grams of nitric acid containing 67.2% of pure HNO_3, will neutralize 54.4 grams of ammonia containing 36% of NH_3?

23. A solid substance contains both a carbonate and an easily dissolved sulphide. How would you prove the presence of these two bodies?

24. Nitrogen may be prepared by using copper clippings, nitric acid and air. It may also be got from ammonium nitrate. Explain the process in each case.

25. Show, from experiment, that (*a*) change of temperature may affect the chemical results when two substances act on each other, (*b*) that the quantities of the two substances may affect the result, (*c*) that the degree of concentration of one or both constituents may alter the substance formed.

26. Describe experiments to show distinction between :—

    (*a*) Finely-powdered charcoal and manganese dioxide.

    (*b*) Carbon monoxide and hydrogen.

    (*c*) Hydrochloric acid gas and sulphur dioxide gas

27. Make the following calculations :—

    (*a*) Percentage composition of washing soda, $Na_2CO_3, 10H_2O$.

    (*b*) Formula of a substance that yields the following percentages of elements on analysis :—sodium, 18·55 ; sulphur, 25·81 ; oxygen, 19·35 ; water, 36·29

28. Indicate methods by which oxygen and nitrogen may be obtained from air.

29. Describe and explain results (a) when dry sal-ammoniac (ammonium chloride) is heated in a test-tube alone , (*b*) when it is heated with quicklime; (*c*) with sulphuric acid.

30. Hydrogen sulphide, marsh gas and carbon monoxide will each burn in air. Write equation for each chemical action. After all water condenses, what will be the relation between the volume of the resulting gas and that of the original?

31. Define dibasic acid. Give an example, and show that the definition applies to the example. Write the salts possible with the bases $NaOH$, $Ca(OH)_2$, $Fe(OH)_3$, and carbonic acid.

32. Three stoppered glass cylinders are said to contain separately carbon dioxide, hydrogen sulphide and nitric oxide. How might the gas in each jar be determined?

212 QUESTIONS AND EXERCISES.

33. How much oxygen will be necessary to just complete the combustion of 4 litres of acetylene, 4 litres of marsh gas, 4 litres of hydrogen and 4 litres of hydrogen sulphide. What volume of gaseous products will remain in each case; all measurements at standard?

34. Mention four ways in which water can be decomposed. Point out in each case what evidence there is that the water is decomposed. State what products are formed.

35. Show how the oxides of nitrogen illustrate the law of multiple proportion. Give the proportions by weight, as percentages, of the two elements in each compound.

36. Iron pyrites, FeS_2, burns in air to ferric oxide, Fe_2O_3, and sulphur dioxide, SO_2. Write equation. What is the proportion by weight of pyrites to oxide of iron?

What weight of caustic soda, NaOH, will the SO_2 from 100 lbs. of pyrites neutralize?

Would a dilute solution of the sodium hydroxide require a different amount of SO_2? (Fe=56, S=32, Na=23, O=16.)

37. It was once thought that the gas set free when zinc is treated with hydrochloric acid was a part of the metal. What reason for thinking otherwise now?

38. (*a*) The residue, when chlorate of potash is heated until the oxygen is driven off, is treated with sulphuric acid

 (*b*) The residue, when oxygen is prepared from chlorate of potash and manganese dioxide, is treated with sulphuric acid

 (*c*) The residue, when carbon dioxide gas is passed through caustic potash solution until the latter is neutralized and the liquid evaporated, is treated with sulphuric acid.

 (*d*) The residue, when acetylene is prepared from calcium carbide and water, is treated with sulphuric acid

What will be the chemical action in each case? Write equations.

39. If 10 grams of zinc were acted on by excess of sulphuric acid and the gas that comes off burned, what would the products of

combustion weigh? If the gas had been collected what would it have measured in litres, at 20°C and 800 mm. pressure? What weight of H_2SO_4 would be required to complete the chemical action with the zinc?

40 Determine the percentage of oxygen in air from the following data.—

15 cc of air were passed into a eudiometer over mercury. Hydrogen was added until the gases measured 28 cc. After standing awhile a spark was passed through, and 19 cc. of gas remained. What was the composition of this remaining gas?

41. Ten grams of dried caustic soda are dissolved in one litre of water; 22 cc. of this solution are required to neutralize 5 cc. of HCl solution. Find the strength of the HCl solution in grams per litre of water.

42. A solution of hydrochloric acid measuring 13 cc. has nitrate of silver added to it until all precipitation ceases; the precipitate after being washed and dried weighed 7·5 grams. What was the strength of the acid in grams of HCl gas per litre of water?

43. A hard glass tube weighed 47 34 grams, a piece of sodium was put into it and the two weighed 49 64 grams; a current of chlorine was passed through the tube and it was heated. When the chemical action was completed the tube and contents weighed 53·19 grams. Find how much chlorine unites with 23 grams of sodium.

44. Give illustrations of oxidation and deoxidation from ordinary domestic operations of the household.

45. Sodium hydroxide, sodium chloride, sodium chlorate, sodium nitrate, sodium sulphide, sodium carbonate are treated separately with sulphuric acid. State the chemical action in each case. What conclusion about the re-placing power of sulphuric acid as compared with other acids?

46 How many grams of sodium carbonate must be taken to yield 10 grams of sodium nitrate? What volume of CO_2 would be set free in the operation? What would this gas weigh?

47. One gram of a certain metal sets free 935 cc. of hydrogen gas from dilute sulphuric acid. What is the equivalent of that

metal? If its chloride has the formula MCl_2 what is its atomic weight?

48. A substance consists of carbon oxygen and hydrogen, a determination of its composition gave carbon 40%, hydrogen 6 67%, density 29·5, approximately Find a formula for it.

49. State Avogadro's law and show its application in establishing the proposition that the density of a gas is one-half its molecular weight, ($H = 1$).

50 In the manufacture of soda water, which would be more economical to use for preparation of the carbon dioxide gas, the bicarbonate of soda or the neutral carbonate, assuming that the selling prices of the two are the same? If the selling price of the bicarbonate were $65 per ton, what should the neutral carbonate cost that they might be equally valuable as measured by the proportion of CO_2 given off?

Make a list of at least six substances of economic importance that are obtained from coal. Bituminous coal rather than anthracite is used for open grates because of the flame it gives. What is this flame due to? What is its luminosity caused by?

51. What information is given by the use of the following chemical formulas —

    (*a*) HCl for hydrogen chloride?

    (*b*) NaCl for sodium chloride?

52. Give names to the substances represented by the following formulas —

$CaCl_2$	$ZnSO_4$	$NaClO_4$	$Al(OH)_3$
SbH_3	$CaSO_3$	KNO_3	$CaCO_3$
Al_2O_3	$NaHSO_4$	$NaNO_2$	$KHCO_3$

(Ca = Calcium.   Sb = Antimony   Al = Aluminium)

53. (*a*) What will be the weight, at 30°C and 750 mm, of one litre of a gas whose molecular weight is 71?

    (*b*) What volume of oxygen, at 25°C and 750 mm., could be obtained from 100 grams of potassium chlorate?

$$(K = 39, Cl = 35\ 5, O = 16\ )$$

54. (a) What is the law of multiple proportions?
   (b) Show that the following analyses of two oxides of sulphur illustrate this law —

	I	II
Sulphur	50 0	40 0
Oxygen	50 0	60 0
	100 0	100 0

55. Write equations for the following re-actions :—
   (a) Hydrochloric acid on manganese dioxide ;
   (b) Sulphuric acid on sodium carbonate ;
   (c) Sodium on water ;
   (d) Sulphur dioxide with oxygen in presence of platinum black ;
   (e) Water on nitrogen trioxide

56. (a) Describe the properties of hydrogen sulphide and a method of preparing (i) a jar of the dry gas, and (ii) a solution of it in water.
   (b) Why is paper which has been moistened with a solution of a lead salt blackened by hydrogen sulphide?

57. (a) Describe one method of preparing nitrogen monoxide, sulphur dioxide, hydrogen chloride and ammonia.
   (b) Write the equations for the re-actions involved.

58 Write equations for the following re-actions :—
   (a) Hydrochloric acid on zinc ;
   (b) Sulphuric acid on sodium chloride ;
   (c) Chlorine on water in sunlight ;
   (d) Hydrogen peroxide on sulphur dioxide

59. A handful of wood ashes is covered with water and let stand for an hour, then the mixture is filtered, and the filtrate changes red litmus solution to blue. (1) What conclusions may be made from this? (2) If some acid were dropped into the filtrate what would be the result?

60. If air is 20% oxygen what proportion of air should be mixed with (a) hydrogen, (b) carbon monoxide, (c) marsh gas, (d) acetylene to make the most explosive mixture in each case, the products of combustion being CO_2 and H_2O?

INDEX.

A.

Acetylene, 150
Acids, 58, 60, 90
Acids, basicity of, 61.
Acids of chlorine, 174
Acid, hydrochloric, 165
Acid, nitric, 102
Acids of nitrogen, 101.
Acids of sulphur, 183.
Acid, sulphuric, 184
Acid, sulphurous, 183
Acids, strong and weak, 202
Action, chemical, 40.
Air, composition of, 86, 189
Air, impurities of, 189
Alchemy, 2.
Allotropism, 55
Amalgams, 27, 111.
Ammonia, 107.
Ammonia, composition of, 115.
Ammonia, test for, 113.
Ammonium, 111.
Ammonium hydroxide, 112
Anode, 15.
Application of Avogadro's Law, 74.
Aqua regia, 166.
Atoms, 18, 193
Atomic theory, 1, 18, 203.
Atomic weights, 23, 206.
Avogadro's Law, 73

B.

Bases, 58, 198
Basicity of acids, 61.
Beginnings of chemistry, 203

Before chemistry, 1
Bleaching by chlorine, 164
Bleaching by sulphur dioxide, 180.
Bleaching by oxidation, 53, 58, 164
Bleaching powder, 170
Blowpipe flame, 160

C.

Calculation of formulas, 116, 188.
Carbon, 123.
Carbon, occurrence of, 123
Carbon, compounds of, 128
Carbon, uses of, 127.
Carbon dioxide, 129.
Carbon dioxide in air, 135
Carbon dioxide, uses of, 136
Carbon monoxide, 140.
Carbon, oxides of, 128.
Carbon, reducing power of, 137.
Carbonates, 131
Carbonates, uses of, 136.
Carbonic acid, 131.
Carbonic oxide, 140.
Catalysis, 147.
Chemical action, 17, 40.
Chemical calculations, 79.
Chemical change, 4, 5
Chemical equivalent, 61.
Chemical nomenclature, 62.
Chemical notation, 37.
Chemism, 20.
Chlorate of potassium, 172.
Chloric acid, 173.
Chlorine, 160
Chlorine, bleaching by, 164.

Chlorine, oxides of, 174.
Chlorine, tests for, 165
Chlorine, uses of, 175
Coal gas, 152.
Combination, chemical, 5
Combustion, 81
Composition of air, 86
Composition of ammonia, 115.
Composition of hydrochloric acid, 167
Conditions that promote chemical change, 11
Conservation of mass, 206

D.

Dalton, J. 203
Decomposition of water by electrolysis, 15, 24
Decomposition of water by metals, 33
Definite proportions, 76, 205
Density of gases 144
Density of sulphur vapor, 185
Displacements. 41.
Dissociation, 197
Dissociation in solution, 198
Dissociation, electrolytic, 201.

E.

Electric charge and valency, 201
Electricity, 15.
Electrode, 15
Electrolysis, 25, 201
Electro-negative, 15
Electro-positive, 15
Elements, 21.
Elements, list of, 22, 206
Empirical formulas, 118
English and metric measures, values, 207.

Equations, chemical, 39.
Equivalent, 68.
Ethylene, 150

F.

Flame, blowpipe, 160.
Flame, luminosity of, 153
Flame, structure of, 155.
Formulas, 38
Formulas, calculation of, 116, 188.
Formulas, empirical, 118.
Formulas, graphic, 121
Formulas, rational, 121.

G.

Gases, density of, 121.
Gas volumes, law of, 206.
Graphic formulas, 121.

H.

Halogens, 160.
Harmonicum, chemical, 30
Heat promotes chemical action, 13.
Hydrates, 59
Hydrochloric acid, 165
Hydrochloric acid, composition of, 167
Hydrochloric acid, tests for 169.
Hydrogen, 26-36
Hydrogen, preparation of, 35
Hydrogen, peroxide (dioxide), 52.
Hydrogen peroxide. uses of, 53
Hydrogen sulphide, 181.
Hydrolysis, 202
Hydrolytic dissociation, 202.
Hydroxides, 59.

I.

Impurities of air and water, 189.
Ions, 199
Ionization, 198.

INDEX.

K.
Kathode, 15.

L.
Lavoisier, 3
Law, Avogadro's, 73
Law of conservation of mass, 206
Law of definite proportions, 205
Law of gas volumes, 206
Law of multiple proportions, 205
Law of reciprocal proportions, 205.
Light and chemical change, 14
List of elements, 22, 206
Luminosity of flame, 153.

M
Mass, conservation of, 206.
Marsh gas, 148.
Metals decompose water, 33.
Methane. 148
Metric and English measures, 207.
Melting, 9.
Mixture, 5, 6.
Molecules, 18, 192.
Mortar, 133, 135.
Multiple proportions, 100
Multiple proportions, law of, 205.

N.
Nascent state, 56
Nitrates, 106
Nitric acid, 102.
Nitric acid, tests for, 105.
Nitric acid, uses of, 107
Nitric oxide (dioxide), 95
Nitrogen, 90.
Nitrogen, acids of, 101.
Nitrogen and hydrogen, 107.
Nitrogen and oxygen, 92
Nitrogen pentoxide, 100.
Nitrogen peroxide, 100.
Nitrogen trioxide, 98.
Nitrous oxide (monoxide), 93.
Non-metals, 22
Notation, chemical, 37

O.
Olefiant gas, 150
Oxidation, 49
Oxidation by chlorine, 163
Oxidation by nascent oxygen, 58.
Oxides of carbon, 128.
Oxides of chlorine, 174.
Oxides of hydrogen, 47, 52.
Oxides of nitrogen, 92
Oxides of sulphur, 179.
Oxygen, 142
Oxygen and hydrogen, 92.
Oxygen, occurrence of, 46.
Oxygen, preparation of, 47.
Oxygen, tests for, 45.
Ozone, 54

P.
Percentage composition and formulas, 116.
Phlogiston, 2.
Physical change, 3
Potassium chlorate, 172.
Precipitate, 15.
Priestley, 3
Proportions, definite. 76
Proportions, multiple, 100.

R.
Radicals, 67.
Rational formulas, 121.
Reciprocal proportions, 205.
Reduction, 49
Reducing by hydrogen, 50.

Reducing by carbon, 49, 137.
Replacement of hydrogen in acids, 67.
Reversible chemical actions, 200.

S.

Safety lamp, 149.
Salts, chemical, 58, 61, 198.
Sodium amalgam, 27.
Solution, 7, 200.
Steam, composition of, 72
Strong and weak acids, 202.
Substitutions, 28.
Sulphur, 176.
Sulphur, acids of, 183
Sulphur and hydrogen, 181
Sulphur dioxide, 179.
Sulphur trioxide, 180
Sulphur vapor density of, 185
Sulphuric acid, 184
Sulphurous acid, 183
Symbols, 23.
Synthesis of water, 70.

T.

Theory of chemical action, 17.
Theory of dissociation in solutions, 200
Theory of nascent state, 56.

U.

Uses of Ammonia, 114
Uses of bleaching powder, 171.
Uses of carbon, 127
Uses of carbonates, 137
Uses of carbon dioxide, 136
Uses of carbon monoxide, 143
Uses of chlorine, 176
Uses of hydrogen peroxide, 53.
Uses of nitrates, 107.
Uses of oxygen, 46.
Uses of sulphuric acid, 185.
Uses of sulphur dioxide, 180

V.

Valency, 61
Valency and electric charge, 201.
Valency, table of, 66.
Values of English and metric measures, 207
Ventilation, 135.
Vital force, 16.

W.

Water, 24.
Water, impurities of, 189.
Water, synthesis of, 70
Weak and strong acids, 202.
Weights, atomic, 23

www.ingramcontent.com/pod-product-compliance
Lightning Source LLC
LaVergne TN
LVHW020515141025
823433LV00005B/191